July 2009

Carol – I hope this book contributes to your journey in a positive way!

Whoever Is There Decides ...
and Other Strategies for the Prevention of Siblingcide™

Virginia Stretcher and
Sally Stretcher Grumbles

Copyright ©2007 Virginia Stretcher and Sally Grumbles.
Editing, formatting and cover by Your Writing Partner,
www.YourWritingPartner.net.

All rights reserved. No portion of this book may be reproduced in any form without written permission from the author/publisher.

LCCN: 2007924429
ISBN: 978-1-59872-853-8

For more information or additional copies, contact: Info@WhoeverIsThereDecides.com or order directly from the website.

Printed in the US by InstantPublisher.com

Dedicated to Mother and Pop

With deepest gratitude to Roy
and Tyler, who made the
journey with us!

Thank you to those others who joined with us
along the road and lightened our load.

Virginia and Sally

Virginia Stretcher grew up on the West Coast. She went to college in Oregon, where she worked her way through a bachelor's degree and found her calling as a history and English teacher. She obtained her master's degree from the University of New Mexico, and settled in California. She had married and was divorced when she went to work for Cox Communications. They moved her to Atlanta to head up their educational outreach efforts working with schools in the U.S. and U.K. When Cox transferred her to the West Coast, Virginia found her way back into public education in San Diego, where she continues to make her home.

Sally Stretcher Grumbles attended college in Mississippi, but met her husband, Roy, in Bakersfield, California. They married in 1972 and moved to Atlanta for Roy to finish physical therapy school (and for Sally to be in the South, which she dearly loved). Sally became a speech therapist, completing her master's at Georgia State University. She then became fascinated with business and embarked on a long career at BellSouth and Cingular Wireless in Orlando, Atlanta and Athens, Georgia. She retired as a Cingular VP in 2003, and continues to reside in Atlanta doing training, consulting and speaking. Sally and Roy's son, Tyler, graduated from the University of Central Florida in Orlando and is pursuing a career in sports management.

Foreword

Our story is not unique. We are two baby boomers born to "greatest generation" parents. We remember our first TV, on which we watched *Howdy Doody*, *Mickey Mouse Club* and *American Bandstand*. We sang along with Elvis, the Beach Boys and the Beatles. Raised on the West Coast, we believed that our generation had received a torch and that we could change the world. We still do.

Like others of our generation, we are members of a club that we didn't want to join. Through a stroke, Parkinson's and Alzheimer's, our "greatest generation" parents were robbed mentally of their senior years and we became "caretakers" before we realized it.

That's why we feel qualified to give advice on the topic of caring for aging parents. We experienced it for more than 20 years in approximately 15 different facilities on both sides of the country, and we made every possible mistake.

To give you some background: Days before Tyler (Sally's son) was born in 1982, Mother had her first major stroke. She continued to have small strokes and developed Parkinson's. She was in a nursing home for a time and had several hospital stays. We were very active in her medical issues, but Pop was primary caregiver.

When Pop's Alzheimer's began to manifest itself in the

mid-nineties, we moved both of them to an assisted living home in Sarasota, Florida (their retirement city). When Mother had her next major stroke a couple of years later, we moved them to Orlando, where Sally lived. Mother stayed in three different nursing homes and was hospitalized twice before she passed away in 1997. Pop was in an Alzheimer's group home.

A year after Mother's passing, Sally was transferred back to Atlanta by her company, so we took turns going to Orlando on weekends to try to keep Pop in that home for familiarity's sake. But finally it was obvious that one of us *had* to be closer by, so we moved Pop to a home for Alzheimer's in San Diego (Virginia's hometown). He was also hospitalized on a couple of occasions during those years. When he required full nursing (he also had developed Parkinson's), we moved him to Atlanta—mostly for economical reasons. He didn't know us, became mostly silent, and was wheelchair-bound in his last years. But he was never bedridden until the last few weeks of his life. He died in 2005, and we had his military funeral with full honors the day after Tyler graduated from college. And so the circle of life continues . . .

This book was written to help others who have joined this "club." If you have siblings or other loved ones involved in your parents' (or other relatives') care, you probably should join the Society for the Prevention of Siblingcide (SPS)™. You may be among the many who have considered siblingcide (mentally doing away with your siblings when they offer advice and orders but little or no help in caring for your ailing loved ones). If you have had these thoughts, welcome. You have passed the initiation process. As the founders and creators of SPS, we sisters, Virginia Stretcher and Sally Stretcher Grumbles, compiled this list of strategies, tactics and action items we used in dealing with our aging parents and, most importantly, with each other.

Don't try to research SPS—we made it up. We realized very early in our dealings with our parents' illnesses that we were getting angry at the disease and taking our frustration out on each other. We still do, and the techniques still help.

This is not a how-to book, but a maybe-this-will-help book. As with any journey, of course, not everyone travels the same path at the same time and in the same way, but we hope you'll find solace and assistance in these pages to help you and your siblings live long, happy lives as family and friends after your parents are no longer around to referee.

Table of Contents

Introduction 1

SPS STRATEGY 1:
Whoever Is There Decides — with No
Second-Guessing, No Blame, No Shame 9

SPS STRATEGY 2:
Make the Tough Decisions Sooner Rather than Later 19

- When neighbors or friends report concern, take
  action quickly 19
- When making the care-home decision, pay more
  attention to "who" than "what" 20
- Hospitalization will happen — it's not your fault 29
- Professional help is not your job, and it may be
  the best choice for your loved one. 30
- Evaluate the facilities 39

SPS STRATEGY 3:
Assume Your Siblings and Other Caretakers Are
Doing Their Best 43

- Every person is doing their best with what they
  have experienced up until this moment in time 43
- Do what you're good at 46

SPS STRATEGY 4:
Care for the Caregivers, Tend to the Caregivers,
Make Sure the Caregivers Feel Appreciated 53

- Caregivers are not servants 53
- Take candy and flowers to the caregivers first 56
- Validate the feelings of your siblings
  (or other caretakers) in their role 60
- Caring for the caregiver 63

SPS STRATEGY 5:
Family Is More than the People You Are Related To 67

SPS STRATEGY 6:
Martyr Is as Martyr Does 77

- Remember who the primary caretaker is 77
- Get an objective and honest business assistant
  and relinquish the financial tasks 79
- Have regular sibling meetings separate
  from holidays 82
- While parenting the parent, don't fail
  to parent yourself 82
- Reach out to others 84

SPS STRATEGY 7:
Whoever Is There Decides — The Cornerstone for the
Siblingcide™ Prevention Society 93

Resources 99

Appendix 101

Introduction

Once upon a time ...

We sure wish this were a fairy tale about two sisters who resided 2000 miles apart and yet together found heartwarming solutions for their aging parents and never fought or cried over those solutions. Sisters who thought the other was making *fabulous* and rational decisions about their own lives and the progression of their parents' lives. We could make it into a TV series and have 30-minute stories with "they lived happily ever after" endings.

Whoops! Unfortunately, this is not a fairy tale—it's the story of our life with aging parents. It is a sometimes funny, sometimes agonizing, and sometimes relationship-threatening account of sisters whose parents needed medical care and attention at an escalating pace.

But before we move ahead, we'd like you to meet Mother and Pop: Lois and Bob Stretcher.

Whoever Is There Decides ...

Pop grew up in Portland, Oregon, with his sister and parents. His father was the secretary for the Portland Board of Education.

He attended the University of Oregon, joined the National Guard, and fought in World War II with the Army in the Pacific.

After he died, we found out (from a letter he wrote to his father) that he had the opportunity to return home but gave it away to "one of the guys who has a wife and family." He was shot a few months later (in 1944), sent back to the states, forced to give up the Army as a career (a disappointment to him), and later given the Purple Heart. He was sent to Fort Benning, Georgia, to train soldiers, where he met our mother!

Mother grew up in Montgomery, Alabama, one of six children whose father ran his own roofing business. She was the only one of the girls to finish high school. Lois married her high school sweetheart when she was 20, but he died soon afterward of tuberculosis. She then moved to Atlanta, Georgia, and began working for Prudential Insurance.

Meantime, as happened to many women in those days, Mother's boss went off to war and she was offered his job. She spent the war years, as vice president of public relations, in New York City for a while but mainly in Atlanta. That's where she was living (in a penthouse with a live-in maid) when a friend set her up on a date with "a cute captain named Bob."

They had dated only a few months when Bob decided to head back to Oregon and live in the old family farm outside of Portland, which didn't even have indoor plumbing. He told Lois he might come back through Atlanta when he concluded his processing at Fort Benning. She told a friend that, if he did come back, "it would be to marry me."

Then began a silent wait. Ten days went by. She began to think she had been wrong and he was already on the way back to Oregon.

When the knock at her door came, she opened it to see Bob down on one knee, outstretched hat in hand. "Let me take you away from all this," he said.

"Let me grab my hat," she answered.

And that was pretty much the way they lived life. He would say "Let's go," and she would say, "Let me grab my hat." (She later added "and the girls.") They were never happier than when traveling or moving to a new town or just out riding. Pop told stories and mother listened and laughed. No matter how many times he told the stories, she laughed.

 **Virginia remembers:** When Pop and Mother first got married, they drove from Alabama to Oregon. They loved to tell the story of buying a bag of chocolate cookies and Mother's pulling them out to eat one or two. Pop was about to drive their jalopy over a frighteningly narrow bridge. She offered him a cookie and he said, "Let me get over this bridge first." She continued nervously munching. When they got over the bridge, he said, "I'll take a cookie now." She reached in the bag and realized that, in her terror, she had eaten them all. We know the story because it was part of the family legends. Pop told the story over and over and Mother laughed every time.

When Virginia was born, Bob went back to college. Four years after Virginia, Sally arrived. The family moved to northern California, then southern California, then back to Oregon, then back to southern California, and on and on. Sally went to nine different schools before she got out of 12th grade, but Virginia beat her record by attending 13.

The moving was tougher on Virginia because she was always president of some club or in a school play, and making good grades in most of her advanced curriculum classes. Sally was usually leaving behind the final exam or term paper on which she was probably going to get a *C* or *D*. (Luckily, she graduated later with a master's degree.)

Our family wasn't perfect—heck, it wasn't even close. We moved constantly and, financially, we were often in bad shape. Mother had a difficult time being away from her family, and Pop felt tremendous pressure to succeed financially while he "found his calling." As a result, with the exception of a yearly summer visit to our grandmother in Oregon for us girls, and trips to the south with Mother to visit her huge clan, our "family" was just the four of us.

Both Virginia and Sally inherited some brains—and some drive—but what we appreciate most of all is inheriting our parents' positive attitude! Mother stayed positive even as the strokes destroyed her sharp mind. She told us once, "The great thing about this disease is that I can read the same books over and over and never remember how they end!"

Mother was an administrative assistant in the federal government when she retired, and Pop was an agronomist for Northrup King Seed Company when he retired a few years later. They moved to Lake Martin, Alabama, in the late '70s and then to Sarasota, Florida. They loved to socialize with their Shrine Club, eat dinner in a restaurant, go to the beach, visit family and friends—anything active and social.

Pop walked five miles a day, and together they drove the vicinity when it was their night on "neighborhood watch."

Our story really begins as their health issues started to affect their ability to continue all the things they loved. But their spirits remained extremely strong through the end of their days. Even when Pop had no idea of his own name, he still smiled, said hello, insisted he felt fine, and never failed to say "Please" and "Thank you." Mother beamed at her caretakers and continuously showed gratitude. She had only a handful of lucid conversations in her last three years, but somehow she exuded a strength that touched everyone.

Mother's final journey spanned six long days, through which we sisters sat in vigil. She actually took in no food or water for nine days. We got to know and appreciate the services of hospice in those days as they educated us on this normal process of passing, which Mother did in May 1997.

Pop's passing was a different story. Though he had had Alzheimer's for over 11 years, he suddenly became sick with pneumonia and, before Sally could even get her things together or Virginia could make travel plans, he was gone. We are pretty sure that St. Peter and Mother came into his nursing home in October 2005, and said, "Bob, let us take you away from all this," and he said, "Let me grab my hat."

Whoever Is There Decides ...

and Other Strategies for the Prevention of Siblingcide™

Thoughts and Notes to Yourself

Whoever Is There Decides ...

SPS STRATEGY 1:
Whoever Is There Decides—With No Second-Guessing, No Blame, No Shame

Whoever is there decides is a simple concept to explain, but a very difficult one to implement. Think about negotiations: If you want A and your parents want C, you can compromise with B. Right? Wrong! Remember that we're talking about your parents; they will never want C, they will always want Z. And they will not understand compromise when it involves their having to change. This negotiation phobia gets worse as they become older and begin to lose control of the world as they know it

A new journey now begins: A situation has occurred involving your parents that requires emergency action. Ours started with a phone call from Sarasota. Pop called while we two sisters were together in Atlanta awaiting the birth of Sally's only child—Mom and Pop's only grandchild. The bad news? Mother was in the hospital after suffering a serious stroke. Virginia left for Sarasota immediately, leaving Sally with Roy and her friends to handle the birth. The choice of who did what was made by Fate.

Pop was not an enthusiastic decision maker about health issues, so that left Virginia to work with the doctors and nurses. Pop allowed her to handle all the treatment plans for Mother while Sally gave birth to Tyler.

Sally remembers: One of the last witty things our parents did was in 1982. Pop continued to have his faculties for a while, but the sharp wit was disappearing. Mother had already been debilitated from strokes. But I had Tyler in 1982, and he was the apple of everyone's eye. The rest of us ceased to exist. Roy and I were mere sidebars to Tyler. That Christmas, Mother and Pop could not wait for us to open a certain gift. They handed us three boxes and told us to open the small one first. It was a little t-shirt with "Tyler" printed on the front. We laughed even harder when we opened the boxes for Roy and me. We also had t-shirts—one read "Mother of Tyler" and the other read "Father of Tyler." There were also "Grandfather," "Grandmother" and "Aunt" of Tyler shirts.

The Stretcher family's journey of tough decisions had begun. While it would take over 20 years (Tyler was born days after that first stroke of Mother's and he graduated from college the day before Pop was buried), the family dynamics had shifted with these two events: Mother's stroke and Tyler's birth. Virginia and Sally were now in charge.

While our parents' lives continued on their way, we had many commitments to others and little extra time to spend with them. Virginia lived on the West Coast and Sally lived on the East Coast. Fortunately, we communicated (though sometimes loudly), but we had lots of love for our folks and each other.

We also possessed high quantities of the three *H*'s: Honesty, Humor and Heart; and the two *L*'s: Loved ones and Luck; and we fought to acquire the big *F*: Forgiveness (for the wrong paths we took along the road and the wrong words we uttered).

We took turns visiting and counseling our parents, and each helped out and, of course, others helped both of us out. Since we were both story-tellers and story-lovers, we most often thought of our experiences as some sort of tale—sometimes a comedy, often a tragedy—and developed strategies and tactics to help us through. This is what we share with you here.

We've actually forgotten when "whoever is there decides" first emerged, but it became a central SPS (Siblingcide™ Prevention Strategy) for us. As issues arose, we came to realize that "letting the other decide" was the key to our relationship during those difficult times.

One time the East Coast sister, Sally, had to decide on a care-home for Mother on one day's notice; another time, the West Coast sister, Virginia, had to put family belongings in a storage area that would only hold a portion of them. Our parents' world, and ours, was changing quickly and relentlessly. We somehow learned, knew, were guided or were told that we had to trust each other. If we spent time second-guessing everything, our support structure would become a house of cards and topple at the most minor gust of wind.

In a "whoever is there decides" relationship, the primary (and perhaps only) role of the ones who are **not** there is to say, "Good choice." Or "Bless you for making that decision by yourself." Or "That's exactly what I would have done." Or "What can I help you with from here?" If you have alternative opinions, you should do the legwork, handle the logistics, and insure that you are present at the next decision time.

More advice to the siblings not present: Give your brothers or sisters credit (more about this later). They will do the best they can, and sometimes after massive negotiations that can involve your parents, your parent's current wife or husband, your parents' siblings, sometimes even your parents' parents, the doctors and medical caregivers, and on and on.

You may think the decision should be Z, but your sibling only managed to get the parent to X. If the negotiations started with A, then X is a miracle; if you want Z, go start the negotiations again yourself.

One of our friends, whose sister and brother live within a few minutes of their parents, ran into this situation. Our friend lives across the country from his family. The brother and sister had begun negotiating to take the car from their dad because he had had multiple accidents. Dad brought it up with his across-the-country child. "I'll only drive in the neighborhood," he promised. What would you say? Remember, it's your parent pleading with you. Our friend thought it would be OK and agreed with his father. Only after talking to his sister and brother did he realize that, in one phone call, he had unraveled months of negotiations. With hindsight, he realized what he should have done: tell father, brother and sister that he supported whatever decision they had made together.

When the sibling "at home" has to decide, make no mistake—it's agony. They must bear the brunt of the day-to-day responsibilities. If, on top of making the decision, they also have to include you in the negotiations with countless phone calls, juggling opinions, researching at your direction, etc., it's a recipe for disaster.

If the nearby siblings know they can evaluate the information available, make a decision, and then call and get your support and praise, you have given them and your parents a multitude of gifts:

1. Your siblings can go ahead and get a decision behind them, which will help them (and you) sleep and function better.

2. They can spend their energy researching and tending to your parents instead of agonizing and foreboding over what you might say to them or your reaction.

3. They can call you and ask for your advice and counsel without risking a controlling dictator on the other end. They will know that a phone call with you will be supportive and loving, and will cheer them up instead of deflating them.

4. You may be better informed about a situation if the risk of another argument is gone. Imagine spending a day with healthcare issues, emergency rooms and your parents, and then having to call someone for their opinion. Imagine instead spending that awful day and knowing that, when you call your siblings, you will receive kindness and support.

5. You have prevented your exhausted sibling from spending minutes mentally creating your punishment, or as we call it, siblingcide™.

The caregivers in the eight nursing facilities we used for our parents were united in the observation that "You are the most supportive sisters we've ever seen, and you never put us in the middle."

Virginia once came to visit the East Coast area where

Sally and our parents resided. A decision had been made about Mother that Virginia was unaware of. She sat in on a planning meeting and commented that a certain situation should be handled in a particular manner. When the social worker uncomfortably advised, "Your sister told us to do it this other way," Virginia said, without a moment's hesitation, "Enough said. If Sally said to do it that way, that's the way it should be done. Let's move on."

Virginia told Sally later that the nursing home staff all stared at her as if she had produced a fistful of thousand-dollar bills. "You mean just like that?" they asked.

"Yep, just like that," Virginia answered. "Sally was here and she decided. If there are decisions to be made today, *I'll* make them and she will support *me*."

And, just like everywhere else, the staff of that nursing center became our greatest allies. They did things like:

1. One of the nurses had seen us reading to Mother from *Chicken Soup for the Soul*. We chose that book because it entertained us, was uplifting, and fed Mother positive thoughts as she went along her final journey. We had no idea whether she heard anything; she was completely unresponsive during those days.

We went out to eat dinner on the day before she passed away, and returned to find this nurse sitting beside our dear mother reading the book to her!

2. Another nurse at that same place had known instinctively that it was very important to Sally to be with Mother as she passed on. So, one evening during the vigil, the nurse stopped Sally as she was starting to leave and said, "I wouldn't go tonight. I'm cleaning her up and then you should come back in." Her words were firm. She put Mother's finest silk pajamas on her, brought Sally back in

and gently said, "She's going." Sally was able to hold Mother in her arms as she passed from this world—looking as grand as possible (which would have pleased her).

3. A nurse who knew that their facility demanded mobility wound up riding Pop around on his walker seat so he could stay there until the last possible moment and we had found another appropriate place.

4. Another nurse adjusted Pop's cleanup schedule because Virginia had arrived late at the home after a cross-country flight. This was quite an imposition on the nurse because it's difficult to keep on schedule anyway and Pop was totally dependent. But the nurse was being supportive of Virginia.

Very simply, we sisters tried to let each other deal with the situations as they arose with our parents, because we were usually alone during our visits. We did share a common vision of concern, of course: we wanted our folks to be happy and safe. We believed that the other sister was doing the best she could to find a happy and safe solution. Interestingly, we sometimes felt that Mother and Pop were our adversaries in this quest. Our challenges were often with them as they coped with their changing circumstances. We allowed, "Whoever is there decides" to be our gift of support.

Whoever Is There Decides ...

and Other Strategies for the Prevention of Siblingcide™

Thoughts and Notes to Yourself

Whoever Is There Decides ...

SPS STRATEGY 2: Make the Tough Decisions Sooner Rather than Later

When neighbors or friends report concern, take action quickly.

Pop was an adored figure in the neighborhood. He loved to build and putter with the tools in his garage, which opened right onto the street. The whole neighborhood could see him working and organizing and whistling at the same time. The children found him patient and enthusiastic about their projects or interests. One of Mother's favorite stories was of the child who came to the door and asked, "Can Mr. Stretcher come out and play?"

The neighborhood parents came to trust and delight in Pop and the time he took with their children. The kids didn't mind that he was forgetful. What adult isn't?

Something different started to happen in 1995, however. Virginia said it best at a later time: "Do you ever forget your keys? That's annoying and can even point to a senior moment if you realize it after you have locked your doors, but it's not dementia or Alzheimer's. When Pop began to forget what the keys were *for*, when he looked at them and asked, 'What are these?' we knew it was a sign of a serious problem. But, like all good children, we managed to overlook it."

Then we got our wakeup call. Mother had become very fragile and Pop was her primary caregiver. Their neighbor called Sally to let her know that he had found Pop in the driveway, just sitting in the car. Mother was in the house resting while Pop had left to run an errand. When the neighbor approached, Pop laughed and said that he didn't know how to get into the house (though the garage door opener was on the visor). He was even confused about where he was. The neighbor immediately called Sally. We were lucky that our folks had such neighbors. Pop's doctor told us to immediately move the folks into an assisted care facility.

Neighbors and friends will not contact you until the situation is serious. The last thing they want to see is a beloved companion moved against his or her will. So be aware that, when they do contact you, they are concerned (or alarmed!) and action must be taken as quickly as possible. We waited longer than we should have to call the doctor, but we soon saw the next tactic on our journey and we never forgot it:

When making the care-home decision, pay more attention to "who" than "what."

Our first lesson about healthcare homes was that the staff is more important than the décor. As in any company, the culture of these care centers starts at the top. When you review the environment, make your first interview with the director. If they impress you as sincere, caring, involved, smart and experienced, the rest will likely follow.

Because of the variety of difficulties our folks experienced, they lived in almost every sort of environment. These care-homes began when Mother had her first stroke, and they intensified as Pop showed serious signs of dementia.

Mother had arteriovenous malformation (AVM), a congenital problem that manifested through an aneurism at age 65. Her stroke was followed by several small strokes that left her unable to care for herself. Pop cared for her and adored her through an incredible number of episodes until his own Alzheimer's made it impossible. Mother needed regular medications, and he had been administering these. When we began to find notes on his calendar and lists on his dresser, we knew he had been working incredibly hard to stay in control while his memory deteriorated. It confirmed that we were doing the right thing by moving our parents to an assisted living facility.

As your parents' world becomes more unmanageable for them, they will try to make it smaller. If they are retired with little to do, a small situation might become a "crisis." One "crisis" for us was shipping china to Virginia. Virginia could have stipulated that she would handle packing and sending the china when she next visited, but soon it reached the fretting stage for our parents. Sally got some good advice from a counselor: Do not solve all of your parents' crises. They enjoy having something to fret about, and a solution might cause a need to escalate their worries. If you solve it for them, they will have two problems to replace it: They now have to (1) find a new problem, and (2) begin the fretting process around that.

We left this problem for our folks and they finally, happily, shipped the china, making friends with FedEx, and other delivery folks along the way.

Virginia remembers: Since Pop loved ice cream, when I would come to visit, I'd take him for a cone as part of our excursion. One time, in the ice cream parlor, he looked at me and said," Where's Mother?" I was stunned. He didn't know me and hadn't spoken of Mother in a long time. I explained that Mother had died. He looked at me in shock.

"Where's Dad?" he asked. At that moment, I realized that he was talking about *his* mother and father. I explained that Granddaddy—his father—had also passed away. He looked more stricken. He asked, "Where's Ginnie?" (his sister), and I had to tell him that she had died too.

As he processed that information, he became a young boy again, and I had just told him that he was an orphan. I reminded him that I was there and Sally was nearby. When I bought him some Chocolate Chip Mint ice cream, his favorite, his fears and pain disappeared and his world was again tranquil.

The assisted living facilities provided good meals, administration of medication, and help in every way for our folks. Because they were organized and alert, they also provided safety and, more importantly, information. Don't underestimate the huge service a care-home can provide by helping to make your decisions clearer, yet kind ones for your loved ones.

**Virginia remembers:** As we've said, Mother's first major stroke happened in Sarasota just as Sally was giving birth to Tyler in Atlanta, and I went to be with Pop. Mother was in a coma and the doctors gave us hope for a full, but long, recovery. To aid Mother in coming out of the coma, the medical staff suggested familiar noises and scenes, so I had the television in her room connected and played CNN and old movies—the background sounds of home. In addition, Pop and I gathered pictures and put cards on the wall.

Many years before, at a political event, Mother had her picture taken with Ronald Reagan. He signed the picture and Mother carried it in her wallet for the rest of her life. She even had copies made, which she shared with everyone. So, Pop took the picture and had it made into a poster for Mother's hospital room. It hung there prominently as Mother was coming out of her coma. During one of her doctor's visits, he turned to Mother, pointed at the picture and said, "Lois, I recognize you, but who is the man?"

Without pausing, Mother said, "Why, that's Ronald Reagan." She didn't know Pop or us at the time, but she knew Ronald Reagan. This became a shared family story.

Pop loved cars. His first car was a Ford jalopy he bought in 1934 for only $5 because it didn't run. Pop and his buddies fixed it up and painted it red with white polka dots. They did this by first painting the car white. Then they traced dots on newspaper with a coffee can, used Vaseline to attach the newspaper dots, and painted the rest of the car red. The result was legendary. He and his buddies even drove from Oregon through Baja, California, in that car.

Pop's love of cars fed story after story. He polished, cleaned, tuned and drove mechanics crazy. So losing his driving privileges must have been very painful for him. But it ultimately revealed what a loving individual he was, even toward a car! The assisted living facility called Sally one day early in Pop's stay to say that they were worried about liability every time he left with Mother in the red car. He was exhibiting Alzheimer's symptoms, and Mom was too deeply into dementia to tell him if she had any concerns. Sally lived in Orlando, but decided she had to face this issue square on. And, most importantly, Virginia was in full support of anything that had to happen.

Sally remembers: I had a business card from the man who had sold Pop the red station wagon and I planned to see if he would sell it for them.

On the Friday following the facility's call, I left work and started the drive to Sarasota. I called from my mobile phone and told my parents that I was on my way. Before we hung up, I said, "Pop, we need to talk about the car. Your new place has transportation and will take you and Mother wherever you want to go. It's probably time to give up the car."

He seemed a bit bewildered. "What do you mean?"

"Oh, Pop, we'll talk about it when I get there." I hung up and began to cry.

I cried most of the way to Sarasota (about a three-hour drive). I cried for all the exhaustion, for how much I missed their humor, for all the sadness in front of us, for having such a great sister and husband and son and friends and job. Mostly I cried because Pop's love affair with cars had to change.

Finally I glanced at the passenger seat with that business card on it and remembered I needed to call the man at the car place. When he answered, I told him who I was. He said, "Well, what do you know? Your father called me not an hour ago and asked if I could sell his car for him. Said it was time. I guess he's bringing it over tomorrow." I could hardly speak. When we hung up, I cried some more out of relief and joy.

When I got to their place, the keys and all the Volvo's paperwork were neatly organized on the table. Pop was his usual enthusiastic self—talking about "the guy" who was going to sell the car for him. The next day, he and I

> took the Volvo in and Pop had a great time with "the guy." He never once mentioned grief or pain. It was just one more time he showed that, no matter where his brain was headed, he would always be a dear, dear soul.
>
> I cried all the way back to Orlando.

The assisted living facility finally had to address the deterioration of our parents' ability to care for themselves in that environment. Mother kept having small strokes, and Pop became more and more agitated because of his dementia and medications. Finally, Mother's third major stroke forced us to move our parents to Orlando to be in the same city with Sally. Mother spent time in nursing homes, while Pop went into a small home environment in a nice neighborhood. It had a full-time care staff—only five residents—which was a comfortable fit for Pop. The difference between the care-homes once again reinforced the tactic of "pay more attention to who than what."

Sally had had no time to systematically evaluate available nursing homes for Mother and, while the décor was beautiful in the first one we chose, the staff was inexperienced and downright clumsy. After Mother ended up with a broken hip, Sally embarked on a new home search, paying more attention to who than what, and was able to move Mother to a very good place. She ended her days in comfort among caring and loving staff.

Pop eventually had to be moved to the West Coast with Virginia, who also remembered the tactic of "who, not what." He stayed in a wonderful home for Alzheimer's patients for years. When he finally needed a wheelchair and true "nursing," the economics drove us to think a move back to the South made sense. Fortunately, Pop loved to travel and these moves did not take much toll (on him). Sally invoked the "who, not what" tactic again, and Pop spent his last few years in a caring environment. As the years went by, we were relieved that we had been able to see to it that Pop was safe and happy. It was important to us that he still heard the voice of joy in so many parts of his life. We hoped that it was because the people in his environment were the types he himself would have chosen.

Think about healthcare facilities as you would a hotel when traveling. Is it clean? Perhaps the rooms are small, but are the common rooms wonderful? Is the food acceptable? Does everyone smile a lot? What do the other people's families think? Are you welcome day or night?

Look at the institution as if it were a school for your children. Seek out the same kind of information about competence. In addition, think of your involvement as you would at your child's school. Buy your parent's favorite kind of cake, but be willing to share. In fact, buy treats and small gifts just to give to the care providers.

As you would join the PTA, join the groups sponsored for you by the facility! Every facility has a support group, or can direct you to one. This is a lonely journey — go where others are in the same boat. One day they will rescue you; the next day you will rescue them; some days you will all just cling to that life raft.

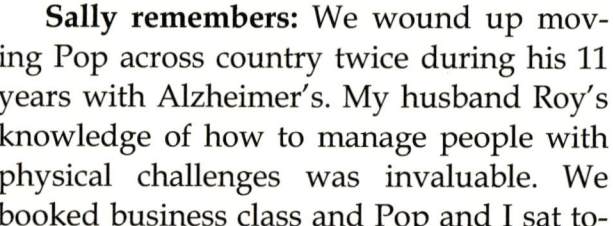**Sally remembers:** We wound up moving Pop across country twice during his 11 years with Alzheimer's. My husband Roy's knowledge of how to manage people with physical challenges was invaluable. We booked business class and Pop and I sat together, with Roy across the aisle. When we flew from Atlanta to San Diego, the Delta flight attendants were fabulous. Pop still had some ability to communicate (though he would pretty much lose it within the next year), and watching them serve the meal fascinated him. They would pull a tray out from the cart, peel off the cover, and set it down in front of a passenger. Pop leaned over to me and said, "You know, this is great. Look at how many people are here and how fast the waitresses are getting them served. Sally, this is a great business. You should think about starting a business like this!"

I smiled and said, "Pop, we're on an airplane," and pointed out the window at the billowing clouds. His mouth formed an *O* and his eyebrows shot up. He peered out and nodded.

About five minutes later, he leaned over to me and said, "You know, this is great. Look at how many people are here and how fast the waitresses are getting them served. Sally, this is a great business. You should think about starting a business like this!"

Ah, the conversations of Alzheimer's!

Hospitalization will happen – it's not your fault. Get mad at the illness but not at those trying to help – including you and your siblings.

Even in the best of places, a loved one can get sick and need greater care than you or the facility can provide. Mother's bouts were more dramatic, but Pop also had to be hospitalized. Do not go through this alone, and don't blame the facility.

> **Virginia remembers:** I got a call from the Alzheimer's facility saying that Pop had been sent by ambulance to the hospital. Because of a black stool, the facility was concerned about internal bleeding. Thank goodness, it turned out to be the result of a change in vitamins, but I was grateful that they had been paying attention. On my way to the hospital, I called a friend of mine with her own medical experience. Her grown son had survived serious cancer at a very young age, and I needed her expertise.
>
> The hospital was wonderful, but Pop was frightened and confused. He didn't know what was happening and he really didn't know me as his daughter. The doctors wanted to perform tests, and Pop was not going to cooperate. My friend was asking questions and we were trying to translate everything. Those few days were stressful to say the least.
>
> Another time, Pop had to be hospitalized for a few days as they adjusted his medication. Just as I had during Mother's stroke, I tried to communicate with everyone at the hospital. If someone came into Pop's room, I tried to engage them in conversation. It made me feel less alone,

> and I gained valuable information. Keep your eyes open and don't be afraid to ask silly questions. Your attitude will affect their attitude. You can point a lot of fingers and get mad at others and yourself, but that won't cure anything.

Professional help is not your job, and it may be the best choice for your loved one. Institutions can be your ally.
Most of us have heard stories of places with poor care, but we found that to be the exception. There is lots of opportunity to do research about care facilities. For the most part, people who work in this industry are competent, helpful, genuinely concerned about their patients and amazingly cheerful. Remember, these people have parents and siblings too. There is respect and, many times, real effort to maintain the dignity of their elderly charges.

Unfortunately, many illnesses rob our loved ones of their ability to understand. They become angry at you and at those who care for them. This is where you must help the caregivers realize that you recognize the anger for what it is — rage at the illness.

Roy (Sally's husband and a physical therapist) constantly advises people not to take care of loved ones at home past the time where it makes sense. Lifting and transporting continuously without help is almost impossible, and so is keeping your health and sanity! Your loved one will get more out of seeing you visit in your sane mind than seeing a wild-eyed, multitasking creature with back problems trying to care for them at home.

In addition, isolation is never good. It's wonderful when you have the resources for round-the-clock care for your parent, but if he or she has to stay in your home, they are still isolated from other personalities and scenes. And you, unfortunately, are as tied to the in-home caregivers as they are to your loved one. If they are unable to come to work, you must stay at home.

Many of us placed our children in school to increase their socialization and provide them with access to professionals and peers. Our elders need the same thing. We have an aunt who didn't want to live in assisted care until she had to, and then she loved it. She was sorry she had waited. She was eating well and going places again. She had plenty of "kin" who wanted to help her, but the assisted living facility gave her back some control that she was losing to those who loved her.

Loneliness and isolation are the greatest enemies of mankind. They attack at any age and rob the person of perspective. At Pop's care-home, many eyes were watching and many mouths could talk. Ask the more alert patients and those visiting about the facility. Pay attention. We heard lovely reports from the lucid patients whose bodies had broken down but whose minds were still good. "Your dad laughed at a joke today," "Your dad tapped his foot to the music—he loves 40s stuff," etc. These reports told us that Pop was surrounded by angels.

Again and again, we found that helpers trusted us because we trusted one another and trusted them. Because we didn't second-guess them or each other, we were quite unusual in their business!

Reminders:

1. Visit, visit, visit; look, look, look; listen, listen, listen!

2. Ask questions of your parents' doctors about their knowledge of the care needed.

3. See Resource section (Page 99) for some places to start.

4. Go online and visit "aging" websites or support groups in your area.

5. Ask everyone you know to gather information about places. Do put a filter on the advice, however. Everyone sees things through their own situation. Use your own instincts if the advice seems positive. Filter out all other advice unless it is sympathetic and makes you feel better about your choice. If it makes you feel guilty, listen without absorbing. If you have a need to feel guilty, don't worry about passing on this opportunity. There will be others.

Don't put on blinders for real problems. Thanks to the Internet, you can research information. Many states make their inspection reports and their license information accessible online. You can find out if there have been sanctions or poor reports on a facility. *Consumer Reports* also has a Nursing Home Quality Monitor (www.ConsumerReports.org/nursinghomes).

6. What religious or ethnic considerations need to be considered for your folks? Do they go to religious services every day? Is that privilege available at the facility, or can it be arranged? Many times, ministers, rabbis or other clerics in the area will *really* know the great places because they go to so many — ask some of them where they recommend.

7. Would your parents feel uncomfortable in certain surroundings or with certain people? Do they have language or cultural concerns? Not YOU — your folks!

8. Did your parents like to garden or tend to an aquarium? Even simple things like that can be part of the facility.

9. Do your parents like to socialize? While at the assisted living home, Mother would sleep in and Pop would

go for the communal breakfast in the large dining room. He and some of the other men would discuss whatever was current. As Mom's illness made her less able to communicate and travel, Pop could socialize without going out. Those may have been his last days of remembering and storytelling. We are so grateful that he was where it was safe.

10. Don't feel the need to follow a traditional path. Our choice for Pop in Orlando was a house with a small number of other dementia patients and full-time care. This was a new concept at the time, but was perfect for Pop. We figured that he just thought he had moved again! As always, these caregivers, patients and their families became our extended family. So much so that, one time, Sally took Pop to visit one of the other patients who had gone to the hospital with a broken leg.

Later, Pop was in a care-home just for Alzheimer's. As his mobility decreased and his need for nursing care increased, we moved him into a nursing facility with mixed patients. Do the best you can and, if it doesn't work, be flexible.

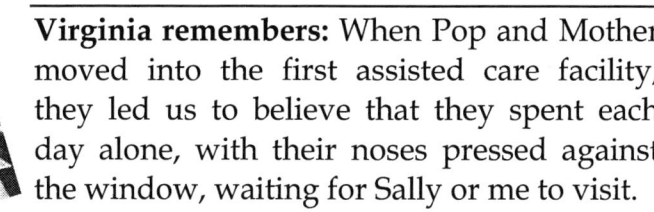

Virginia remembers: When Pop and Mother moved into the first assisted care facility, they led us to believe that they spent each day alone, with their noses pressed against the window, waiting for Sally or me to visit.

One day, I went with them to an afternoon dance. As they were dancing, one of the other residents smiled and said, "Your folks love to dance; they are here for every dance and every time there is music, they dance."

They were missing us, yes, but their days were filled with activities and people. Your folks will say things to

> try to recreate the world they loved, the world where everyone was home together, the world when you needed them. It may be that they are trying to recreate their energy and activity. They are missing who they were as much as they are missing you. Tell them you love them and remember a story of their youth together, but don't try to solve their sadness for them; it's part of the process. Sally and I reacted and overreacted, but it was all due to that guilt (the gift that keeps on giving).

11. If you have a regular workplace and regular hours, a home close to your work may be a good choice. You can visit *occasionally* on your lunch break or after work. If you are the only sibling in the area, try to make your visits unscheduled. It helps to reduce expectations from your parents and the facility.

12. If you have a large, extended family with children and grandchildren who will visit, ask them to stay only 15–20 minutes. Short, but frequent, visits are a good solution to visitation. Just stop and have a cup of coffee. It makes them feel loved, but it doesn't overwhelm you or them. Short visits at first can also protect you from your own sadness. If there is a regular activity that a sibling or family member likes, such as bingo or the sing-along, let that person go during that activity and take your parents. Sometimes your folks might be reluctant to go alone, and would probably be thrilled to have a family member/friend join them, and the activity takes the pressure off to chat.

13. Consider using the same pharmacy used by the facility. There may be additional costs involved, but if your parents need medication in the middle of the night—even cough syrup—using the facility's pharmacy may save you a trip to the drugstore and to the facility. It can also speed

delivery and provide better care.

14. No matter which pharmacy you use, ask them to package prescriptions according to dosage. This can begin while your parents are still living independently. The drugstore can halve the pills and put them in individual plastic bottles, or even create morning, noon and night packaging. This procedure prevents the risk of improper or forgotten dosages. It's also a great help to the medical people in the facility, and can be important for your parents' medical issues if the facility has changes in personnel. As with all medical people, they are friends and allies. They want your parents to have the best care and will support you. Laws of privacy today can be tricky and you may need your parent's permission to even call the pharmacy. If so, find out from the facility which medications your parents are taking.

Virginia remembers: While in California, Pop needed a change in medication. Changing required that he check himself into a facility that could monitor the effects. The most wonderful nurse sat with us and tried to explain what was happening. I could tell that Pop was getting scared by the terminology, but she calmly continued to work with him. My job at that moment was one of trust. I realized that Pop was taking his cues from me. I listened and nodded. As I put on a good face, he relaxed and she could do her job. That is your job—to listen. Do the best you can but let go and let the professionals do their job. Remember, you have several stresses—your parent is sick and you have become the parent. Stay alert but, if you have chosen a facility you trust, let go!

Whoever Is There Decides ...

15. Consider the facility's location:

(a) Is there fast food nearby where you can grab a treat for your parents (or yourself)? If they used to love Wendy's, take them a "picnic." There is usually a cheery common room to eat in. If your folks are lucid and want to talk, great! If not, bring a videotape and watch a movie together. Buy tapes or DVDs of favorite movies for the facility too, and ask the activity director to show them and invite your parents and others. Sharing is good.

(b) Is there shopping nearby for family and friends visiting from out of town? If your folks need new clothes or personal items, having a store close by makes it easy to take a break and handle the errand simultaneously.

(c) Is the facility close to an inexpensive hotel or motel where you can stay?

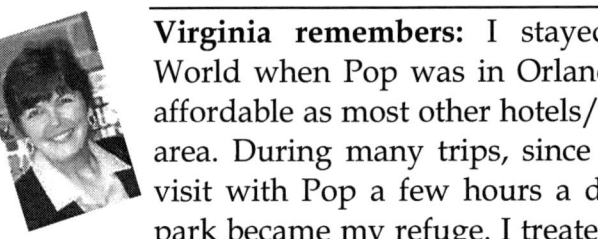

Virginia remembers: I stayed at Disney World when Pop was in Orlando. It was as affordable as most other hotels/motels in the area. During many trips, since I could only visit with Pop a few hours a day, Mickey's park became my refuge. I treated myself to a year-round pass. I knew every ride, attraction and character. I felt safe at the Happiest Place on Earth, and it provided something to do while I was by myself. I can remember one summer when the aftermath of a hurricane closed every activity except Epcot's IllumiNations. It was magnificent!

Disney World became a partner with me as I dealt with Pop. Because I was the sister with no children, and got holidays off from my job as a teacher, I spent most of my Thanksgivings and Christmases at Disney World. I

> will always be grateful to Disney cast members for making me feel less alone during those stressful times. They didn't know how important they were, of course. I didn't need to share the pain; I just needed distractions.
>
> Go to a movie, ballgame, rodeo or car race. Find your distraction. Give your grief some time to rest, and build your reserves for tomorrow.

16. Keep up with the paperwork—wills, insurance, Powers of Attorney, Do Not Resuscitate forms (medical people will refer to this as a DNR and it is a common, and sometimes required, form), living wills, etc. Try to get these forms into a safety deposit box with shared signatures of family members. We tried to keep the forms in a safety deposit box near to the folks.

Keep copies of these documents with you as well. Virginia had the Power of Attorney and DNR for our parents. She even carried a copy of those documents in her glove compartment and purse, and there were circumstances when she had to use them. When Pop was sent to the hospital for internal bleeding, Virginia rushed directly to the hospital from work. Those papers got her into the emergency room and, even though all the forms had been filed with the hospital, the staff was grateful that she could produce them for copying.

Sally called several times because facilities for both Mother and Pop required Virginia's release, or permission for some form or medical issue. Sally would fax the form, Virginia would sign it (or write a letter), and fax it back with a copy of the Power of Attorney.

Forms are a part of our world. All facilities will require them. Today a pharmacist can't show you, or even talk to you about, your parent's medication without their permission.

Virginia stored copies of the Power of Attorney and DNR everywhere—even her suitcase. She is still finding them.

Don't believe that a form will solve everything, however. Yes, your mom may have a living will, but that tube might need to be inserted to help her with sustenance during pneumonia. If your loved one deteriorates, removing it will probably require permission of all family members—even the ones you don't speak to.

and Other Strategies for the Prevention of Siblingcide™

Evaluate the Facilities

No facility is going to be perfect, but perhaps this checklist will help. Put a + for a positive "feeling" on this item, a — if you had a negative feeling, and a 0 for neutral. Then compare notes with any other siblings who take the time to do the same. If your parents are suddenly in need of a care facility, take your best guess, go for it, and do research for an alternative later. Whatever you do, don't feel you can't make a change. (There are extra copies of this form in the Appendix.)

Facility 1: _____

Facility 2: _____

Facility 3: _____

Facility 4: _____

Item	1	2	3	4
Outside area for walking				
Director of facility				
Head of nursing				
Inside "look" of facility				
Cleanliness				
Music				
Outings suited for our loved one				
Religious services				
Clothing/possession handling				
Comments in parking lot				
Location of nurse stations				
Resident appearance				
Appearance of rooms				
Smell inside				
Comments of local associations that visit (like Alzheimer's Association)				
Comments of ministers if available				
Nurse focus: residents vs. paper				
"Feel" of residents' "hope"				
Food reports from residents				
Number of visitors allowed				
Proximity, convenience				
Comments of other families				
Feeling of positive attitude				
Variety of fun				
24/7 access				
Your access to staff and other patients				
How medicine is dispensed				
Noise level				
Phone access				
Billing/finance				
Interactions observed				

Whoever Is There Decides ...

Thoughts and Notes to Yourself

p. 33 - parents' reaction to assisted living

p. 21 - parents' crises

Whoever Is There Decides ...

SPS STRATEGY 3:
Assume Your Siblings and Other Caretakers Are Doing Their Best

Every person is doing their best with what they have experienced up until this moment in time.

Those words were on a sign someone gave Sally when she left college. As a speech therapist, she often dealt with parents who denied their children's problems, or refused to help them. This sign helped her forgive and control her anger.

Sometimes people would like to believe that they're not really related to their siblings. One of Virginia's principals used to tell teachers that parents were sending their best kids to school, not hiding the great ones and sending the others. So we say to you: No one is hiding your really wonderful siblings in the basement. These are the ones you have, and they probably want to be great.

If you remember this short phrase, anger and judgment may dissolve, or at least help you deal rationally with the situation at hand. Let's break it down:

Doing their best: Everything depends on your point of view. You may occasionally see someone you perceive as a slacker — someone who does not do their best. But they do do their best—at whatever is important to them. No one really sets out to foul up a job or responsibility when it comes to family.

The second part, *with what they have experienced up until this moment in time*, is the key. Well-known statistics say many abusers come from abusive homes. Think about how they experienced home life—so what experience do they have? This also applies to people from different cultures—they may only know how to respond in a way different from yours. Perhaps this is true even if your "sibling" is a "spouse" instead. Many people were raised differently, especially in matters related to love, death and caring. Patience, understanding and listening are your best tools against siblingcide™.

> **Virginia remembers:** I received a call from a caregiver. She had taken out Pop's dentures and helped him use the toilet. Somehow a denture fell in the toilet and was flushed away. She called me in a panic. I tried to reassure her. After all, Pop needed help to go to the bathroom, and she was there trying to help him—I wasn't. I knew she hadn't purposely thrown it away; it was an accident. And I knew he wouldn't starve; they'd figure out the food situation while I ordered a new denture.
>
> The denture was replaceable—her care and concern for our father was the most important factor. Our understanding helped her to relax and focus on him. Upsetting her could have resulted in poorer care while she fretted about her mistake. As Mother always said, "It's only money."

Many facilities demand regular care meetings, and we found that automatically making the assumption that everyone was doing their best allowed us to save a great deal of time.

Sally remembers: Once, Virginia and I were in a care meeting together. This became pretty unusual as time went on, because we learned that only one of us needed to be at these. That gave the other a break and, in a "whoever is there decides" relationship, it works.

Mother was completely bedridden and hadn't uttered a meaningful sentence in about a year (she just stared happily into space most of the time, showing no recognition of anything). The caretakers were tiptoeing around the therapy they were doing—trying not to admit that they were simply dragging Mother through the motions to keep her muscles somewhat toned. Virginia said, "So do you think we should enroll her in ballroom dancing?"

There was silence as the professionals looked amazed. "And will she be able to play the piano?" I asked, and then continued, "Because she never could before!"

This old joke broke the silence, and the caretakers laughed gratefully. They began speaking about the strength of the spirit coming from Mother and how sad they sometimes got because they knew she would not really improve. They showed confidence in their skills and their caring, and we got honest feedback.

Do what you're good at.

Are you a people person or a numbers-and-facts person? It's important to understand which you—and others—are so you don't force your left-brain, deal-maker sibling to take your loved one to the doctor while you take care of getting a better price at the pharmacy. Be honest about your skills and theirs! And mix or share the duties whenever possible.

In our case, Sally was interested in business and the bottom line, while Virginia was a born teacher and people person. Our parents had given the oldest daughter—Virginia—their Power of Attorney. As it turned out, most of the time our parents were ailing, Virginia was not the one in the area. So even though the business piece would have been Sally's *interest*, it worked out well because Virginia could conduct business from far away. Pop later got a third-party businessperson to take care of the books and bills while he was still able to make decisions, and Virginia managed that person from across the country.

If there are several siblings, we suggest that you sit down early in the process and have a meeting. Everyone should write down what they think they are good at, or what "specialties" they bring to the table, and what they think others are good at. For instance, if one sibling is good at organizing, they need to help your parents organize old pictures and mementos and subtly begin cleaning out the house.

This is no time to get defensive. Remember in the movie *Terms of Endearment* when Aurora said, "Your one gift, Flap, has always been that you recognize your limitations"? This is the time for your family to do the same.

If Mom's favorite is Stacey and everyone always teased or resented Stacey for that, now is the time for Stacey to give back. In the sibling meeting, everyone can acknowledge that Stacey is the one who makes Mom's heart sing. If Stacey lives in town, she can be Mom's primary visitor while the other siblings take on what they are good at. Even in a demented haze, Mom will respond to Stacey best, and what a gift you have given her by just being realistic. Note: The "Staceys" of the world are generally not the money managers and documenters. Don't put Stacey in charge of managing the bills AND visiting Mom. It would be unfair to everyone.

We have provided a tool on Page 49 for you to identify what you are good at, what you like, and what you believe your siblings excel at. Hopefully, the form will include everyone. If it doesn't, or if one sibling seems to have the most checks, use this as an opportunity to talk through the situation. The best form would be for everything to be checked by different siblings!

Sally remembers: Pop was getting pretty ill by 1995. We had finally gotten them moved into an assisted living place, and knew they were OK because the people there were managing Mother's medication and Pop could just socialize. We knew his Alzheimer's was underway, but we resisted seeing it. I would usually drive down to Sarasota on Friday night and back to Orlando on Saturday. I sometimes got a kick out of his memory issues.

I could call on Thursday night and say, "Coming down tomorrow," and he would yell out to Mother, "Say! Sally's coming to see us." Then as I was en route, I would call from my mobile phone and say, "I'm on my way," and he would yell to Mother, "Say! Sally's coming to see us." When I knocked on their door, he would open it, his face would light up with surprise, and he would yell, "Say! Sally's here to see us!"

I told my friends that I got to surprise and please my dad three different times for the same trip.

and Other Strategies for the Prevention of Siblingcide™

Do What You're Good At
(Who is *best* at this in the family? Second best?
Insert initials in those boxes, and then compare notes! There are extra copies of this form in the Appendix.)

Name/Initial _____   Name/Initial _____
Name/Initial _____   Name/Initial _____
Name/Initial _____   Name/Initial _____

Skill	Best	Next best	Skill	Best	Next best
Shopping			Trusted by others		
Negotiating			Running errands		
Following up			Creative activities		
Mom's favorite			Has time		
Dad's favorite			Simplifying information		
Documenting records			Teller/reader of family or other stories		
Security/privacy/computers			Noticing problems/details		
Inspiring others			Calling extended family		
Objective view of family			Visiting/chatting		
Completing what's started			Making difficult decisions		
Crafts/clothing care			Event/occasion planning		
Choosing thoughtful gifts			Medical knowledge		
Making phone calls			Financial planning		
Knowledge of family history			Other business and finance matters		
Legal knowledge			Handling emergencies		
Family comic/entertainer			Other		

Date of family meeting _____
Family member filling out form _____
Location _____

Whoever Is There Decides …

and Other Strategies for the Prevention of Siblingcide™

Thoughts and Notes to Yourself

p. 46 – subtely clean out the house

Whoever Is There Decides ...

SPS STRATEGY 4:
Care for the Caregivers, Tend to the Caregivers, Make Sure the Caregivers Feel Appreciated

Caregivers (especially if they are siblings) are not servants.

Caretakers are not obligated to adhere to your schedule or comply with your wishes. We were amazed at the stories Roy (Sally's physical-therapist husband) told us about people who would ask him to schedule his appointments with their loved ones according to *their* appointments to get their hair done, or people who asked him to haul their garbage to the street "on his way out."

We were equally amazed at what we saw in the nursing centers. Family members would speak to the caretakers in a demeaning or condescending way. They would go on the attack during care meetings, saying things like, "Dad's shirt had coffee spilled on the front during my last visit. Why can't you keep him neat and clean?"

And the worst: They would put the caretaker in the middle of family squabbling. "I told you we would pay for laundry services here at the home. I don't care if my sister says she will take the laundry and do it herself. You do it here!" (We often wondered if siblingcide™ finally occurred in that family.) We even witnessed cases of siblings moving a family member when the other sibling went on vacation, effectively placing the facility in the middle.

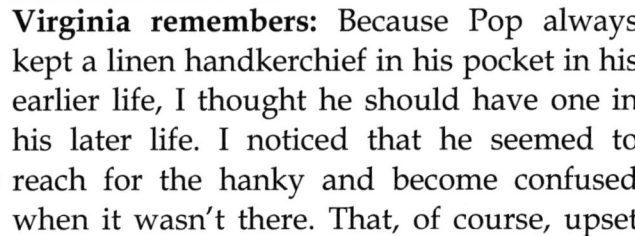

Virginia remembers: Because Pop always kept a linen handkerchief in his pocket in his earlier life, I thought he should have one in his later life. I noticed that he seemed to reach for the hanky and become confused when it wasn't there. That, of course, upset me terribly ... until the day he reached into his pocket and I went to get clean handkerchief. I returned quickly and handed it to him. He took it carefully, then looked at me and said, "What's this for?" You see, it mattered to me because it meant that some part of Pop was still Pop, but it really didn't matter to him anymore—Alzheimer's had robbed him of attaching any meaning to the handkerchief.

The caretakers were wonderful. They were trying to remember the handkerchief for me. Pop might have been dropping it along the way. It no longer had significance to him—only to me.

The role of the therapist, nurse or caretaker is to rehabilitate or keep your loved one comfortable and safe. In most cases, these jobs are not highly paid. If you did your research well in the beginning and found a place with staff you were impressed with, now is the time to give them respect and trust their judgment in most cases.

Do not ask them to do anything to make life more convenient for YOU. To take liberties with John Kennedy's words: "Ask not what the caretaker can do for you; ask what you can do for the caretaker."

If the caretaker happens to be your sibling (or your spouse), take this advice in triplicate. If you are out of town and your sibling is the day-to-day caretaker, NEVER be snippy if they don't tell you about some part of your parent's life. Don't call them any more often than they appear to wish. Instead, call the professional caretakers in the home for an update, or call your parent directly if they are lucid. Then call your siblings so they know they don't have to make that phone call themselves today, or even call you. They will appreciate it.

During our highest stress period, we even stayed in motels instead of with our in-town sibling so she got a true break from all obligations to family while the other one was in town.

If your parent must see caretakers or therapists at home, keep in mind that these traveling healthcare workers have a logistical nightmare. They will call and say, "I'd like to see your mom in 45 minutes." Then they might hit traffic or face a sudden patient or family emergency of their own or almost anything. Try to be very flexible. Be kind and appreciative. Don't ask them to babysit. If they want you to exercise your loved one or check a vital sign or empty a bedpan, find it in yourself to follow the instructions without question and with kindness.

No matter how important you are in your job or life, this person is far more important in the job of caring for your loved one. And healthcare people are different from businesspeople, educators, professionals or laborers. They see disease, pain, hurt and death constantly. This often gives them a peculiar, but endearing, sense of humor. If you are easily offended, don't engage them in too much conversation. And pay attention to the next tactic:

Whoever Is There Decides ...

Take candy and flowers to the caregivers first.

Sending your loved ones a treat to the care-home? Send the same treat to the caregivers. If you can't afford to send full quantities to both, send your loved one half and send the other half to those who deal with the situation daily. We learned this through our own lifetime love affair with See's Candy. See's is abundant in the West, but not easily available in the East. When Virginia visited our parents, she always brought candy and the staff would be invited to share.

We realized how much they loved this unusual treat when they began asking Sally, "When will your sister be back?" We connected the dots, and Virginia started sending candy for any special occasion—a small box for Pop or Mother and a big one for the nurses and aides to share. The caretakers started talking—really talking—to both our parents. They loved the candy, but were happier about the obvious value that we, the family, saw in them. Gradually, we did things like taking a birthday cake for Mother or Pop and placing an identical one in the break room that said, "Thanks for all you do for our folks."

Also remember that there are multiple shifts and multiple jobs. *Caretakers* refers to anyone who has responsibility for day-to-day or night-to-night contact with your loved ones, not just those who nurse them or prepare their meals while you are there. They include nurses, aides, cleaning staff, janitors, pink ladies, and doctors of all persuasions.

Send goodies to all three shifts and label them per shift. The off-hours shifts often see only empty boxes or baskets, and labeling will prevent that. Goodwill is generated directly from you to them to your loved ones. If you don't believe it's an investment in better treatment, you don't understand human nature.

Once Sally wanted to give a party for Pop's 87th birthday. Virginia was coming to town the following month and he would have another celebration, but a party seemed important. It touched Sally when her friends, many patients, some of the attending medical staff, and family members of other patients came by for that afternoon of singing *Happy Birthday* and munching  cake. It touched them to see Sally feeding and patting Pop, and made them feel good to hear him sing a few words of *Happy Birthday* right along with them.

Gift ideas for caregivers (all shifts):
- Candy or food (especially fresh fruit)
- Novelty food items (maybe from their/your area)
- Cards
- Simple gifts (even from dollar places)

Note: Do not give food of any kind to another patient. You don't know their medical history. Give it to the staff to share with other patients if appropriate. Just like your folks, some patients are on special diets, medications or doctor's orders. This goes for many other gifts as well. If your folks are sharing a room, ask the staff about music, videos, flowers, etc. (Remember, whether you take a plant yourself or order it for delivery, ask for unbreakable containers.)

Gift ideas for special caregivers (including siblings and spouses):
- Gift certificates for spas (3-4 times a year). Call the spa, give them authorization to charge up to $X on your charge card, and tell them to make the massage, manicure, facial, etc., as wonderful as possible but NOT to make a pitch to them.

- A year-round pass to a theater, park or even Disney World.
- Gift certificates for ANYTHING they might want to do for themselves.
- Notes of appreciation (jokes or cartoons with a note will count) once a month.
- Meals at a restaurant (3-4 times a year).
- Cards or emails of appreciation (once a month).
- A visit to *relieve* your sibling—no criticism or questions allowed. You take over seeing the loved one for a span of time where it is clear that the sibling caretaker is not expected to appear (3-6 times per year).
- An offer to care for your sibling's children or be there for a holiday so they can really escape (once a year).
- Actual gifts (clothes, books, figurines, videos, etc.) every time you see something they might love.
- Call to say, "Everything looked great to me" within one week of your visit. If something did not look right, take care of it yourself by phone. Then call the sibling caregiver to let them know what you have done.
- Loudly saying, "And [Name] is amazing" at all family gatherings and in the common room when appropriate.

Sharing refers to more than just *things*, though. If you are feeding your loved one at a common table, talk to the others who are feeding the patients—both staff and families. You all may need company, consolation and mental stimulation. Break the silence and they will let you know if they want to talk. Sometimes the family member or caretaker wants to share stories about their patient or loved one; sometimes you'll talk about the weather.

Think of the people sitting at that table as you would think of people feeding babies around a table together. Talking and sharing would definitely happen. Certainly, the atmosphere would be more hopeful, but the camaraderie is still real.

Seek out information about your loved ones from the others as you sit there. Oddly, these people, both families and staff, may know a lot about you and your parents through patient chitchat.

Ask staff members especially where they're from, if they have children, and what they've done in their life.

Pop had caregivers with incredible stories, many from exotic lands. One was a doctor who had immigrated to the United States after marrying. The job was an opportunity to be involved in the medical area while studying for tests to gain her doctor's license in the US. Her job here was demanding, but the issues could be left at the facility when she needed to study. She had never offered her fascinating stories, but through our interest and questions, others at the table learned of her courageous life.

Some people work in assisted living facilities to leave their own loneliness, some love to spend time with elderly people, some feel a calling. As we mentioned earlier, one of the nurses spent her lunch hour reading to Mother in the last days of her life. The nurse later shared that she had had a difficult relationship with her own mother and it was a comfort for her to console ours.

Validate the feelings of your siblings (or other caretakers) in their role.

Do you know how the word *empathy* differs from *sympathy*? Webster's Dictionary says sympathy is "a relationship between individuals in which whatever affects one affects the other in a similar way." Empathy is "identification with, and understanding of, the thoughts and feelings of another." You see, empathy is a deliberate and developed skill. Sympathy is more of a feeling you can't deliberately acquire.

When you grow your ability to empathize, you will be able to validate others' feelings, even though you may not understand them. You will be able to let someone "vent" without getting defensive. You'll be able to see what they are experiencing.

Let's say your sister goes to see your father two times a week. She begins to fret because buttons are missing from his shirt, or a sweater has disappeared, or there is strange underwear in his drawer.

This is not the time to "make suggestions" such as, "Why don't you complain to the director?" or "Why don't you label the clothing?" These comments will only make your sister more anxious and upset.

Instead, say, "It really scares you how much you have on your plate, doesn't it? You know, Dad doesn't know a button is missing, so feel free not to fret." Or "You must be so tired. A kid at home and a full-time job, and then two times a week you race over to be sure Dad is OK. Who cares if a sweater is missing? We just appreciate all you're doing."

This accomplishes a lot. It tells your sister that she is OK and that her emotions are the normal feelings of being overwhelmed. It also tells her that she can call and vent to you anytime because you are really on her side.

The day-to-day sibling may not see changes in appearance as clearly as you do either, because changes are gradual. If you're stunned during your annual visit at how old your parents suddenly look, check out how the primary caregiver looks too!

What NOT to give the sibling caregiver:

- Instructions of what ought to be done.
- Reports of what you wish you could do and what you would do if things were different.
- Chores to finish: "I called and got a list of meds for Mom. You just have to order them and pick them up. This will save gazillions of dollars."
- Instructions to "Just go get the form at the post office and make a photocopy of his military ID," or anything that sounds like that.
- Reports of concerns: "Don't you think the nursing home is getting run down?" Instead, do research for a new place and ask the caregiver for input.

We stumbled on a great idea to help each other through the tough times. At one point, Sally was caring for Mother in the hospital, overseeing Pop in an Alzheimer' home, raising a 13-year-old son, living with a husband who was incredibly supportive but deserved some time, and working a full-time, demanding job. She was scared and overloaded, but didn't want Virginia to feel obligated to move to the East as she had often offered to do.

Sally knew, however, that Virginia was the only one who "truly understood," and one day she called Virginia and vented to her answering machine about how hard all of it was and how discouraged she was getting.

Virginia called back and got voice mail. She left a "poor you" message: "You poor, sweet thing. You have so much going on—all the responsibility, no time for yourself, having to see the folks go downhill and being so helpless. You work so hard and nothing really gets solved. Poor thing. Your plate is overloaded for sure. I wish I could be there to help, and I'll come out as soon as possible to give you a break. I respect you so much for all you're doing—it's amazing. But I know you're just plain tired, you poor, wonderful sister."

> **Sally remembers:** I kept that voice mail for weeks. When I got the blues or became discouraged, I would dial it up and listen. It made me feel valued and understood. And it endeared Virginia to me all the more. When Virginia later had "custody" of Pop, I remembered and left her that same type of validating message. Please remember that this type of kindness works when any sibling, friend or spouse is going through hard times.

and Other Strategies for the Prevention of Siblingcide™

Caring for the Caregiver
(There are extra copies of this form in the Appendix.)

Year _____   Location _____

Family member filling out form _____

Action Item	Date Done
Called to tell them we appreciate what they are doing	
Called to tell them we appreciate what they are doing	
Called to tell them we appreciate what they are doing	
Called to tell them we appreciate what they are doing	
Called to tell them we appreciate what they are doing	
Called to tell them we appreciate what they are doing	
Called to tell them we appreciate what they are doing	
Called to tell them we appreciate what they are doing	
Called to tell them we appreciate what they are doing	
Called to tell them we appreciate what they are doing	
Called director of facility	
Called director of facility	
Called director of facility	
Sent candy or gifts to staff	
Sent candy or gifts to staff	
Sent candy or gifts to staff	
Came to town and totally "relieved"	
Came to town and totally "relieved"	
Came to town and totally "relieved"	
Called parent and then called caregiver to give them a break from making that call	
Called parent and then called caregiver to give them a break from making that call	
Called parent and then called caregiver to give them a break from making that call	

Whoever Is There Decides ...

and Other Strategies for the Prevention of Siblingcide™

Thoughts and Notes to Yourself

Whoever Is There Decides ...

SPS STRATEGY 5:
Family Is More than the People You Are Related To

Speaking of caring for caretakers, don't forget those other caretakers who may be involved—family members of the sibling who is caring from afar and those living with the situation every day right along the sibling onsite. Maybe these are even friends who are "just like" siblings.

> **Sally remembers:** An incredible friend of ours passed away after a lengthy bout with cancer. The mother of his beloved actually sent me a dear note to say how much she had witnessed and heard from her daughter of our devotion and commitment to him and to her daughter. I was so impressed that she actually took time to note our participation and notice our devotion to our friends. Roy and I were so close to them that his passing and the pain that went before was *vivid* for us. That she noted so sweetly validated how far-reaching family can be.

Sit down for a minute and write a list of the family members you feel you can count on. Now make a list of the friends you can count on. Now put those lists together—that is your real family. If there are more friends than actual family, so what? Remember that our "greatest generation" parents counted on more than family. Since we moved constantly, our family was the close friends that our parents made through newcomers' groups and church. We remember our times with them with as much love as we do our time with actual family.

When you are the most stressed, remember the line from *Ghostbusters*: "Who ya gonna call?"

Our greatest ally was Roy Grumbles. He was not our sibling, but became Virginia's through Sally's marriage. Wow, did he get pulled into this world!

Sally and Roy had a short courtship and now have a long marriage. Fortunately, he was able to survive some interesting moments—like every holiday or celebration. He could probably write his own book: a Paul Harvey type "rest of the story."

Virginia remembers: In 1977, our parents decided to retire and move from California to a lake in Alabama. Mother and Pop had always moved themselves, and this was to be no different. Their last move had actually been 14 years before, when they had moved across the city. Now they were moving across the country. We were still young during the last move; now we were married and our husbands were horrified. With Pop's usual optimism and Mother's ability to detach, we were on the verge of a favorite family game: "Let's make an ordeal." Packing was a breeze compared to the actual trip. Sally and Roy were living in Atlanta, but they trav-

> eled to Bakersfield to help with the move. Virginia and her husband at the time helped with the packing and the exit strategy.
>
> We never saw Pop say an unkind word to anyone. Unfortunately, inanimate objects were not given this same consideration. He would curse, yell and kick at things. I'm not sure Roy had ever seen this in action before. But on this move, he saw the stubborn side of Pop and the clinging side of Mother. Pop drove the truck with Roy, and Sally drove the car with Mother. Pop was a risky driver at best, and these were unfamiliar roads. He merrily took every mountain back road he could find, and Mother got sick in the back seat of Sally's car. As a result, Roy was panicked during the day by Pop's driving and horrified by night as Sally cried about Mother.
>
> A tribute to Roy: He actually stayed in the family! Years later, he would be the key in moving Pop across country twice. By then, of course, Pop was deep into Alzheimer's. While I know that Pop no longer remembered that other trip, Roy certainly did—but he went anyway.

A word about appreciating those related to the situation:

Spouses/significant others are having their own experiences and their own stresses. Roy was in the healthcare industry, so he also had knowledge, opinions and experience with caregivers. So he was probably far more helpful to Sally in that role than if he had been in a different profession. But in the most intense years, Roy had to experience Sally's lack of energy and attention to him and Tyler as she gave more and more to the caretaker role. Roy had to pick up most of the parenting of Tyler. (Sally always says, "Of course he was a better nurturer anyhow.") He also was acutely aware that his own family in California was coping with his mother's illnesses and he was not contributing to that as he would like. Showing appreciation to those who are making less-obvious sacrifices (but may be caretaking the caretaker) is a great idea.

Sally remembers: After Mother died, Virginia came to be with Pop for Christmas while Roy, Tyler and I went to Hawaii. It was more a gift to Roy and Tyler than to me, I think, but I was very grateful. She planned a Christmas celebration with Pop by bringing him to our house. She told hilarious stories about it all later.

Virginia remembers: Sally, Roy and Tyler had gone to Hawaii for Christmas for a needed R&R. I went to Orlando from California to spend Christmas with Pop. On Christmas Day, I picked him up from the Alzheimer's home and brought him back to Sally's where I was staying. I had brought and bought presents, but they needed wrapping. Pop had a great time helping with the wrapping and oohing and aahing over all the gifts. We put them under the tree and then I served our Christmas dinner. After dinner, we opened the presents. Even though he had just wrapped them, they were all new to him. As a result, he was thrilled again! It was definitely one of those smiling-through-my-tears moments. I was happy to see him happy, but I sure missed my father.

The children of your sibling caregivers may be experiencing the situation in a unique way. They may not have an understanding of why their mom or dad needs to travel to see family and not take them. They may wish the parent had more time to take them to activities or just be a bit more focused. They may be watching beloved grandparents as they lose humor or precious relating abilities.

Sally remembers: Tyler always was intuitive, smart and sensitive. (Am I biased? Virginia says he is too!!) But from an early time, I was able to talk about reading *Final Gifts* when Mother died and how it related to my faith in God. As the folks deteriorated, Tyler saw me have "melt-downs" when the house was a mess, my work was demanding, and a call from the nursing home came through. He also got to see the beautiful circle of life as he transferred from "cared for" by Pop to "caring for" Pop. We talked about the natural progression of life quite often. And when Pop died, Tyler got the eight-hour trip to home (he was in college) underway quickly, but he was not scared and knew he would find everyone to be OK.

Tyler had benefited from lots of time with his dad (he became an Eagle Scout—something worked on by dads as much as boys). And he was able to experience (1) his mom and dad caring deeply for his grandparents, (2) his mom interacting with her sister in a supportive rather than antagonistic fashion, (3) his grandparents having a normal "aging with illnesses" experience with support of family surrounding them, and (4) his dad supporting his mom in difficult circumstances.

Whoever Is There Decides ...

What is key to remember is that the spouse, the grandchild or the nephew also has had a relationship with the aging relative—they too are feeling the sense of loss in that important relationship. In addition, they are experiencing some learning and some loss in their own immediate families. Care for them too. Spend time and energy on them.

When you need help and support, call your friends. If you say something in anger that you really shouldn't have said out loud, your friends will likely have a shorter memory than your siblings. Your siblings remember when you wet your pants at the age of four; your family knows your buttons. Your friends pretend not to notice—that's how you know they are your friends.

> **Sally remembers:** As you're gathering allies, also consider the professionals.
>
> When we moved Pop from Orlando to San Diego, and from San Diego to Atlanta, we used a ground troop of allies. First and foremost was Delta Airlines. Virginia and I had both flown Delta for years for business and were familiar with the planes. The first trip required a plane change in Atlanta. Even though Pop was somewhat mobile, Roy and I arranged for a wheelchair in case of a possible time constraint. That also gave us an extra set of hands. (Remember to tip everyone!)
>
> Everything was set at the Alzheimer's facility, but we were unsure of Pop's reaction. We arranged for a car to meet us at the airport. Virginia had the car pick her up at the facility in San Diego and she was waiting at the airport. This may seem like over planning, but Virginia is a schoolteacher and her view was that this was the greatest of field trips, so we tried to cover all the possible problems. We believed that having a car and driver would free us to focus on Pop. It is also a great gift that is "only money" but might save your sibling's sanity if a trip like this is necessary.
>
> The return trip several years later had fewer variables because, ironically, Pop was much more fragile. We were lucky because Pop was a happy traveler.
>
> **NOTE:** This was before September 11, 2001. The logistics are different, but over planning is still the key.

Your friends will amaze you. Your family will amaze you. Both sisters had friends and family who took up the slack when we were unable to move forward. Or sometimes they just said, "You're not crazy" or "You should be so proud."

Many of you may know that, as you age, extended family becomes critical. We reconnected with cousins (who are usually a cross between friend and family) and attended family (and friend) reunions as often as possible. Family is as family does (a positive spin on the next chapter title). Just let everyone do what they can at that moment. Ask, but be sensitive to the answer or the way it is delivered. Forgive others, as you would have them forgive you. Show appreciation to the support system of the support system.

and Other Strategies for the Prevention of Siblingcide™

Thoughts and Notes to Yourself

Whoever Is There Decides ...

SPS STRATEGY 6:
Martyr Is as Martyr Does

Remember who the primary caretaker is.

Let's get directly to the point. Just because you are taking care of the finances and you call every Sunday from miles away, you are not the primary caregiver!

If you and all your siblings with their spouses/partners are in a restaurant with your parents and one of your parents has to go immediately to the restroom or has an "accident," who goes with them and who cleans them up?

That person, whoever it is (it might be your sister-in-law), is the primary caregiver! You better start taking care of that person and making sure she or he takes care of themselves.

So stop giving that person advice or tasks and start giving them support. Call and tell them how much you appreciate what they are doing. Send them flowers, gift certificates, e-cards. (Hallmark has a free service, and Yo-Yo and Hoops have saved our sense of humor.)

Can you help that person financially? Can you offer to pay for a trip, a massage, a movie trip for the family? Negotiate a way to let them accept it; they will appreciate it and you will feel great! They will begin to realize that you are supporting them while they are supporting your folks. That feeling is what will be remembered when your parents have gone.

Stop for a minute and create this image: For every diaper you change for your parents, you get to give one minute of advice to everyone and they must listen. So change the diaper or keep your advice to yourself.

If you get overwhelmed during your visits from out of town, go sit in the car or run an errand! Take a five-minute break to breathe or cry or get angry, and forgive yourself for this. Play golf, or at least hit a bucket of balls at a local course. Don't let a visit imprison you with guilt.

Reminders:

1. Denial can be your friend. Your heart and mind may seem to break with pain as you begin to accept the inevitable. Let it come in stages—you will accept it as you can. Reach out to your support people; you will be surprised where help will come from (we hope some angel gave you this book). Others have traveled this road; it is part of the healing to help the next person over the hurdles. Listen to their advice and use your instincts.

2. Probably the hardest part for us was the traveling cross-country to visit a parent who didn't even know us. Everyone would talk about the fun of seeing our dad. It wasn't fun—Pop spent the last ten years of his life trapped behind a wall of nonrecognition. This was a man who had gone places and done things, but now he couldn't remember his life or even us. He was unable to care for himself and, for the last few years, he couldn't even walk or stand.

Get an objective and honest business assistant and relinquish the financial tasks.

We know we didn't make every decision perfectly. Make no mistake; we made many errors in judgment. We both agonized about going through our parents' things. There was over eight years between their passings. Normally, Pop would have made decisions about Mother's things with us, but Alzheimer's had taken this ability from him, so it was left to us.

When the folks first moved out of assisted living in Sarasota, Virginia went through things. When she couldn't take any more tears, she took the unsorted things and put them in storage. Much of it was not worth keeping, but the sorting broke our hearts. It took many years to reduce the volume. This simply prolonged the grief and, on top of that, it was expensive to maintain. But you do what you can do and forgive the rest.

Perfect people would have cleared this up about their parents' things and moved on. Well, good for perfect people. You have to do what you can do. The dollars spent on a storage facility may save your sanity at the moment. We sacrificed sorting for time with Pop. But do remove clothing and keepsakes as soon as you can. They are part of the grief that you must let go.

One early decision was really right. We know that not everyone will have this option but, for us, hiring someone who paid the bills and kept the books for Pop (for a surprisingly reasonable amount of money) was a blessing that kept us from additional stress and martyrdoms.

As our parents entered the assisted living care facility in Sarasota, Mother was deep into dementia from strokes and Parkinson's. Where Mother had always handled the money, Pop was now doing the finances and he was entering the first stages of Alzheimer's. We were concerned and inquired at the assisted care facility for suggestions. They gave us the name of someone who was helping other elderly patients. This wonderful lady with her husband, and her secretary were our angels. The husband was a CPA and she specialized in managing elderly customers who were alone or, like our folks, living away from family.

She spent hours with Pop while he was still in the early Alzheimer's stages. She worked patiently with him to see that she had all the information correct. He was able to go with her to the bank to see his banking "friends," and it was obvious that those who had been dealing with him for the last few years had been worried about his increasing forgetfulness. They were relieved to see that he had gotten help.

We were so lucky. Pop had always been a people person and had dealt with the same bank for years. They knew him and he knew them. We kept his money under the care of "our angels" and that bank for the rest of Pop's life. He had trusted them. We trusted them.

We knew very early that our parents had little money. Their house was paid for, Pop's retirement plan gave them some relief for medicine, there were a few small paid-up insurance policies, and Pop received money as a retired Army officer. That was the bulk of their resources. With a little more from Social Security, that was all the money they had to support them for the rest of their lives. We expected nothing, of course. All their money was to be spent on their care. We were so grateful to have resources for that.

We always advise others to have that perspective, and are amazed at decisions that "protect the assets" so Mom gets "as-necessary" provisions while her estate grows. So, when she dies, each sibling gets some share—which also will cause problems. Our advice is to spend on your parents as they would spend on themselves if they had no children. Expect NO inheritance. They gave you life and character; what else do you want?

Early on, we used some money to reimburse ourselves for expenses, but that changed. Airfare, hotels, gifts, clothing, treats for the folks and the facility staff were our expense.

Why is an objective third party best to manage, and advise about, the finances? For one thing, it may be easier for you and your siblings to deal with a third party. Finances are a tricky part of sibling trust. If one sibling takes on the financial matters, two things easily might happen:

1. The others may underestimate how much time it takes to manage even simple financial matters. A small bank error can take hours to undo. Eventually, the one in charge will become resentful that he or she is shouldering all the responsibility. Martyrdom could easily set in.

2. The others may become suspicious or distrustful because they have no control over the money. This is called "human nature," and is no cause for shame.

Trying to share the responsibility between several siblings is even worse! If one sibling is handling the house and another is handling the optometrist, they may not be able to spend money during the same month. If an outsider is handling the money, payments can be negotiated through them.

In fact, your most important issue may be to figure out the assets. Your parents may have money in several banks, in various accounts, or even hidden in the house. It is not uncommon for ailing people to hide money and jewelry for safety and forget it. Mother lost her diamond ring one night. Hours later, we found it in a box in a drawer. She had put it there for safekeeping.

Even if you hire a financial assistant, one sibling must supervise him or her, which, in itself is time-consuming. In our case, Virginia took this on. What we advise is that the sibling who manages the assistant is the one who lives farthest away. As we moved Pop and circumstances changed, we tried to let one sister handle the people issues and one handle the financial issues. Sometimes it worked and sometimes it didn't. But finances can be handled effectively from a distance by phone and computer, with only occasional visits.

Have regular sibling meetings separate from holidays.

Another way to avoid martyrdom is to clarify, clarify, clarify. Who is in charge of what? How do people feel about the financial assistant who was selected? Does everyone respect and trust him or her? Is everyone happy with the carehome? Is anyone jealous or cautious? Is anyone feeling overwhelmed? Or in need of help? Is anyone thinking of siblingcide™?

Since both of us love the seashore, we often met at a beach hotel. We walked together on the sand and then returned to the room to hash out different items—a chief one being the finances and location of Pop. There were tears and arguments and name-calling and hugs, but we got through that treacherous passage pretty well—without resorting to violence.

While parenting the parent, don't fail to parent yourself.

Would your parents have allowed you to go three nights straight with no sleep? Would they have forced you into four full-time jobs? Would they have advised you to let your marriage or relationship falter in order to take care of an ailing relative? If you answered yes, you need different parents. Put them in a home and go see them every six months! Don't worry about them, either; they are busy giving bad advice and annoying others. People who give guilt are equal opportunity givers: whoever is there receives.

But we're pretty sure you answered no, so we ask you: Why are you allowing yourself to get no sleep, work multiple jobs, eat too much or too little, and let your love life wither? Sure, we know there will be times when you can't help giving too much, but try not to be a martyr.

Sally remembers: When Mother was in the hospital with a broken hip, and Pop was throwing fits in his Alzheimer's home, and my son had just split his mouth wide open jumping ramps in Extreme skating, I dropped down in the doorway of the hospital and had a good cry. Then I called Virginia just for comfort. It felt good to talk to her and even better when she moved up her visit to give me a break.

Most of the time, all those unavoidable situations happening at once is the oddity. At times you will get a phone call from a caretaker sibling, or you will be the caretaker sibling making the call. Listen and let the other person be rational for you while you are self-talking your way into a hole.

We put ourselves in double-stress because we *had* to go visit both parents on Valentine's Day (even though one of them hadn't known what Valentine's was in about three years).

Hey, give yourself a break. Go to a movie or a bookstore, run a few laps, eat right, sleep all day, see friends, rent a comedy DVD, play an upbeat CD, plan and take a vacation! Tell the institution's caretakers how much you appreciate their help and that you will only be there once a week for the next month while you prepare for the big presentation at work. Be honest with the people taking care of your parents.

During the week of Mother's final illness, we went to see *Romy and Michelle's High School Reunion*. We thought it was the funniest movie we had ever seen, and we ate popcorn and laughed and laughed. We even bought each other a video of the movie. It wasn't quite as funny later as we remembered, but it was a lifeline at the time.

Take a break. Let the caregivers know you are always available by phone and then live your own life for a couple of weeks! And while we are talking about letting yourself off the hook, here's another tactic:

Reach out to others. When offered help, accept it without being ashamed. If not offered, ask.

But, unless the helpers are being paid, you must not hold them accountable. If it is your sibling or a friend, you must be able to take over the task at any point without resentment.

On our journey, we heard, "If there's anything I can do, let me know" a hundred times. Usually, if we asked for help, we would receive it, but we found that we had to be specific about our needs and limit the number of requests. "I'm going to Florida to help my sister out with Pop. Will you feed my plants until Monday?" Or just be honest about why you are going. It helps others to understand your situation. Ironically, Virginia had coworkers who thought she was just visiting her dad. They had lost their dads and would have been happy to visit him. Unfortunately, a visit to a very sick parent is not a happy visit. You will always gain from the experience, but it's stressful. You may be changing his diaper, making funeral arrangements, or trying to get him to eat. Our father was no longer there mentally. He could not carry on a conversation. For the last few years of his life, we had little recognition from him and only short glimpses of the "real him."

Sally remembers: I had a boss who said, "If there is anything I can do ..." This is tricky. You don't want to miss work or drop the ball on an important assignment. But this boss was sincere and caring (not to mention one of the funniest humans on the face of the earth).

One day, I just plain needed some advice. I thought of my boss. I went to his office and he gestured me in the second he saw my face. I did not cry. Rather, I said, "I need advice. My parents made it clear that they did not want tube-feeding. But Mother can't eat for herself anymore and the home is asking me to state clearly that I do not want tube-feeding. I feel torn; I know this is the end for her unless I get this tube-feeding thing that could make her last many more months."

His memorable advice was this: "Decisions like these require that you ask only two questions: Will this make my loved one get well? If the answer is yes, do it. If the answer is no, ask Question Two: Will this make my loved one more comfortable?" He then told me that he had helped his mother make extremely difficult decisions about his father's cancer treatment. He said, "Question

> One told me that it would not make my father well, but then nothing would make my father well, so I quickly went to Question Two. For our gravest decision, the answer was yes, so we went forward."
>
> I had renewed admiration for him. I asked myself if tube-feeding would make my mother well. Forget it. So I asked myself if it would make Mother more comfortable. The answer was obvious. I told the nurses that I would sign a document telling them not to tube-feed. And, by doing that, I honored Mother's living will. The staff congratulated me later on what they called a difficult, but kind, action. Then they asked Virginia for her permission. At this time, Virginia was on a business trip out of state but, based on "whoever is there decides," she signed because she trusted me (and that wonderful boss). I asked my boss for help, and he gave it. If I had asked every day, however, it would have been too much.

If someone says they will run by and visit but don't, never mention it to them. But if you pay an aide to walk your loved one and they don't show, follow up, follow up, follow up.

>  **Virginia remembers:** During one trip to Orlando, I broke out in hives after taking an overnight flight to take Pop to a doctor's appointment. It was a difficult time—traveling cross-country and feeling so helpless. Pop did not always know me by then and I was feeling very down. So I called Sally from the parking lot of a drug store. I actually sat on the curb and cried into the phone as she tried to comfort me long-distance. There wasn't a solution. His illness was the culprit. Reaching out keeps you from being alone with the pain and stress.

Decisions such as adding tubes, taking a tube out, or even pulling a plug may come suddenly, so it can help if you have already talked with your siblings (and parents). In addition, with today's laws and safeguards, this may not be your decision alone.

You are not by yourself, and this journey is not unique to you. Not only seek help, but let others help you!

Notaries can be found at banks, mailing facilities, realty offices and your place of work. Forms can be downloaded from the Internet, but try not to do this alone. If you are at work, go to your human resources person for help in accessing forms. Many local libraries and volunteer organizations can help as well.

Ask for help for three reasons:

1. To be sure you're getting the right form. You may need their state form and not yours.

2. Others have been where you are going and can give you necessary information, the right questions to ask, etc.

3. If you are doing this long-distance, you may obtain information that can help your sibling or parent who is on-site with the parent. Don't make it an order. Simply say, "I had to go to the library for this form. They made some suggestions that I felt I should pass along for you to evaluate and use at your discretion." Your tone is essential. If it sounds like you are sharing information, they may listen. If it sounds like a to-do item, you will have lost them with "hello."

Reminders:

1. Try not to let anyone take on more than they can handle — even if he or she wants to. Don't let the primary caregiver pay for and handle the medications, do the laundry, entertain the patient, care for the professionals, and do the other daily chores.

2. Try to separate the day-to-day care from the business side.

3. Recognize the financial truth.

4. Be supportive. If this is not possible and you believe that it has to be your way or the highway, put down this book. Either move next door to your parents or into the care facility, or move your folks into your home. Forget this book — you don't have time to read.

5. Practice what you preach and try to model how you want to be treated. If you send your brother to buy your mother a new robe and he returns with a blue one, even though she hates blue, praise him anyway. One of two things will happen: Your mom will love it because he gave it to her, or she will smile at him and complain to you. Either way, she is happy and the problem is minor.

6. Avoid being manipulated. Are your parents pur-

posely, or without recognizing it, pitting you against each other? After all, that was your strategy when you were young and wanted something from them, wasn't it? If you and your siblings are only speaking to each other through your parents, your messages are being manipulated. If you all communicate through one sibling, your messages are being managed. Without any intention of harm or misleading, everyone hears what they want to hear and repeats messages that have been filtered through their set of experiences. Try to get everyone together during a nonholiday time and talk openly.

7. Give as much time to *you* as you do to *them*. Easy to say, right? At the Alzheimer's home in San Diego, one of the spouses said that his doctor had asked him who was going to take care of his wife when he died. That startled him, because it was the wife who was sick, not him. The doctor shared with him the statistical reality: Caregivers shorten their own lives, and some actually die before the patient, because of exhaustion or lack of self-care. Your folks need you, but give yourself as much care and attention as you give them and you will be able to care longer and better for them.

8. Don't make your parents' care a contest. How about this as a rule? The last person to change the parents' diapers wins.

9. Listen to professionals and follow their advice. If they find that you listen to them, they will give you more advice and information. In every place that Pop resided, we felt like part of a team. When we called, we spoke first with the caregivers. We believed them and we watched. If something seemed odd, we checked with each other before we spoke up. If we did speak up, we did so with an open mind: "Is there a reason that Pop is eating only mashed food? Oh,

he's complaining about his dentures, huh? Let me see if I can help with that."

In our feeding-tube decision, Virginia also had to sign the agreement, which needed to be notarized. She visited a community where she had vacationed and went to a local realtor for a notary. These were strangers to her, but not strangers to stress. Recognizing the situation, they sent her to the local library for additional forms that needed to be signed by Sally.

The people at the library not only provided the forms, but also emotional validation for what Virginia was experiencing. They had all been through a similar situation or knew someone who had. There were tears that day, but they were good tears. They washed away a lot of pain.

and Other Strategies for the Prevention of Siblingcide™

Thoughts and Notes to Yourself

p. 82 - finances from a distance

Whoever Is There Decides ...

SPS STRATEGY 7:
Whoever Is There Decides— The Cornerstone for the Siblingcide™ Prevention Society

This strategy has been repeated by others, enjoyed by professionals, and used in odd places like funeral homes and auto-painting shops. We hope it will help you through your challenging times with your parents or other loved ones. But mostly we hope it does for your sibling relationship what it did for us—draw you closer during difficult times and cement your relationship into a strong bond of support for your many future adventures.

Your journey—like ours—continues. You may have signposts of your own. Your parents are scared. Their world is not in their control and they need to trust that you can help them sort out this new world. From beginning to end of this difficult journey, your brothers and sisters are the most important asset you have.

Just as your parents needed to be united, so do you. It is in your family's best interests.

> **Sally remembers:** When we lived in Oregon, we went to the mountains one weekend. We were driving down the mountain toward home when an ice storm hit. The road was steep, curvy and on a terrifying cliff. Virginia and I sat silently in the back as Pop maneuvered to keep the car straight. It was sliding and slipping. Finally Mother said, "I'm going to turn on the radio and we can be distracted by what's on there." She did so and looked for a station. The first one she found was a religious channel playing *Nearer My God to Thee*. Mother and Pop started laughing hysterically, so Virginia and I followed suit.
>
> There it was. The gift we received from our parents was the ability to see the positive and the humor in every situation.

Reminders:

1. Do unto others as you would have them do unto you (or your family's version).

2. Try to understand your siblings first and then your parents. If you and your siblings can agree, your mom and dad may actually relax. They may be scared of the pending changes, and knowing you are a unit circling to protect them may give them needed security.

3. Listen and talk. If you don't understand, say so. But try not to begin with, "That sounds stupid; why did you do that?"

4. Ask the person doing the action and not your parents. If your brother arranged an outing to a flea market, don't ask your parents, "Why are you going there?" Ask your brother. He might want to surprise them and take them

to the flea market's country cooking place that has fried green tomatoes because Mom loves them and rarely has them.

5. Always believe the best. Default to the best intentions.

6. Your sibling is 50, not 5. Stop saying, "You always mess things up." It may be true, or it might have been true a long time ago, but either way, it is not the issue. Good care for your folks is the issue.

7. Try to find a way for everyone to benefit and win.

8. If your family is spread over the country, or even the world, consider the time difference for early morning and late night calls. A sibling on the way to work may not have time for a chat at 8 AM Pacific Time or when you just left your folks' home at 11 PM Eastern Time.

9. When your sibling calls and is upset, stop and think: Is he hurt or in the hospital? Or perhaps she is having a terrible time at work and your mom has called her three times to talk about the cat's fur balls? Give your sibling sympathy, tell them to let you call your mother and listen to her. Then call your mother and listen to her complain about the fur balls. It won't hurt for her to know that your sibling called you with concern about the issue. She knows you care and she knows you will talk to her.

10. Start calling your parent more often. This may be a great way of reaching out. If you live a distance from Mom, you may be able to help with phone calls. This will free your sibling and help you feel less guilty about not being close by. But do not take orders from Mom for your sibling. A follow-up call to your sibling about a need of your mom's may be worse than the fur balls. Remember, fussing is a way of feeling necessary, so let your mother or dad fuss.

11. Stop and think when your sibling calls and accuses you of something out of your control. What in the world prompted this call? Say, very calmly, "That's awful; I'd be upset too if it were true. Whoever told you that must have misunderstood." Never accuse another of bad intentions. Try not to fall into "he said, she said."

12. If there is bad news, call immediately. If you think you may have acted foolishly or need a sanity check, call immediately. Don't wait for your sibling to hear anything through your family's grapevine. No matter what, the gossip will always be worse than what actually occurred. That is the beauty of family.

13. Start calling your family for no reason at all and at odd times. Call and talk about a shared remembrance that made you smile and will make them smile. Tell your siblings that you are thinking good thoughts about them. If you feel comfortable and mean it, tell them you love them. Ask forgiveness for an old hurt. Expect nothing in return. You could be working on years of catch-up. It will be OK. You and your siblings will survive these changes.

Hurts and repairs of hurts, private jokes and shared heartbreak or joy is how family is created—our family, extended family and your family.

The important message is that generations move on. If you don't really share the experience and insist on being a "lone wolf siding with good old Mom and Dad," you deny yourself a celebration of true family—those who believe in you and love you and share your time on Earth.

Our parents have now passed on; you might be at a different stage with yours. Were we perfect? Hardly! Did we do our best? We hope so! Did we learn a lot on the journey? Absolutely! We have acknowledged how important it is to forgive ourselves, to forgive each other, and to move on. We want you to have access to our experiences for what they are worth, and we hope they will prevent a few mistakes along your journey.

Is our relationship better? Yes. For better or worse, we are family. We know our lives were enriched by these painful, joyful, exhausting, exhilarating, ordinary and extraordinary experiences and the people whose lives we intersected along our way. We wish you luck and joy along yours.

Whoever Is There Decides ...

and Other Strategies for the Prevention of Siblingcide™

Resources

This is by no means a comprehensive list—just some of the websites or information sources we found helpful and/or have been referred to us along our journey. We also avoided giving too many specific references and stuck with broad information categories to serve as some places to start your own personal research journey.

Websites:
National Council on Aging: There is so much information here that it can get you started on your way to finding answers about almost any topic on aging, illness, communication, etc. www.ncoa.org

American Association of Retired Persons: A vast amount of information in their magazine and their resources. www.aarp.org

US Department of Health and Human Services: Information and advice on every topic imaginable, including Medicare and hospice. www.hhs.gov

Consumer Reports occasionally reviews nursing homes and healthcare options, and does not accept advertising. When they do reviews, they suggest valuable evaluation tools to help you as you look for the best care. www consumerreports.org

Our website:
In addition to providing ways to order this book, the family-meetings forms in this book are available for you to print and, as we become exposed to more resources, we will strive to make them also available. www.whoeveristheredecides.com

Books:
We found few books as we began our journey, but there are far more of them now. As we embarked on writing this, a friend remarked that there will be full sections in bookstores devoted to this topic as the population ages. A favorite on the topic of understanding the language of the dying is *Final Gifts* by Callanan and Kelley (two hospice workers with enormous common sense and empathy).

Disease-Based Organizations:
Support groups abound for most far-reaching diseases, such as the Alzheimer's Association, Kidney Foundation and Cancer Society. Find one in your area of need and be sure you are following up with a large and reputable organization. Be aware that, once they have your email information, you may receive more fund-raising efforts than you want. But they all give you "opt out" opportunities.

Good luck on your journey!

APPENDIX

Feel free to make as many copies of these forms as you need.

Evaluate the Facilities

No facility is going to be perfect, but perhaps this checklist will help. Put a + for a positive "feeling" on this item, a − if you had a negative feeling, and a 0 for neutral. Then compare notes with any other siblings who take the time to do the same. If your parents are suddenly in need of a care facility, take your best guess, go for it, and do research for an alternative later. Whatever you do, don't feel you can't make a change.

Facility 1: _____

Facility 2: _____

Facility 3: _____

Facility 4: _____

Item	1	2	3	4
Outside area for walking				
Director of facility				
Head of nursing				
Inside "look" of facility				
Cleanliness				
Music				
Outings suited for our loved one				
Religious services				
Clothing/possession handling				
Comments in parking lot				
Location of nurse stations				
Resident appearance				
Appearance of rooms				
Smell inside				
Comments of local associations that visit (like Alzheimer's Association)				
Comments of ministers if available				
Nurse focus: residents vs. paper				
"Feel" of residents' "hope"				
Food reports from residents				
Number of visitors allowed				
Proximity, convenience				
Comments of other families				
Feeling of positive attitude				
Variety of fun				
24/7 access				
Your access to staff and other patients				
How medicine is dispensed				
Noise level				
Phone access				
Billing/finance				
Interactions observed				

Evaluate the Facilities

No facility is going to be perfect, but perhaps this checklist will help. Put a + for a positive "feeling" on this item, a − if you had a negative feeling, and a 0 for neutral. Then compare notes with any other siblings who take the time to do the same. If your parents are suddenly in need of a care facility, take your best guess, go for it, and do research for an alternative later. Whatever you do, don't feel you can't make a change.

Facility 1: _____

Facility 2: _____

Facility 3: _____

Facility 4: _____

Item	1	2	3	4
Outside area for walking				
Director of facility				
Head of nursing				
Inside "look" of facility				
Cleanliness				
Music				
Outings suited for our loved one				
Religious services				
Clothing/possession handling				
Comments in parking lot				
Location of nurse stations				
Resident appearance				
Appearance of rooms				
Smell inside				
Comments of local associations that visit (like Alzheimer's Association)				
Comments of ministers if available				
Nurse focus: residents vs. paper				
"Feel" of residents' "hope"				
Food reports from residents				
Number of visitors allowed				
Proximity, convenience				
Comments of other families				
Feeling of positive attitude				
Variety of fun				
24/7 access				
Your access to staff and other patients				
How medicine is dispensed				
Noise level				
Phone access				
Billing/finance				
Interactions observed				

Evaluate the Facilities

No facility is going to be perfect, but perhaps this checklist will help. Put a + for a positive "feeling" on this item, a − if you had a negative feeling, and a 0 for neutral. Then compare notes with any other siblings who take the time to do the same. If your parents are suddenly in need of a care facility, take your best guess, go for it, and do research for an alternative later. Whatever you do, don't feel you can't make a change.

Facility 1: _____

Facility 2: _____

Facility 3: _____

Facility 4: _____

Item	1	2	3	4
Outside area for walking				
Director of facility				
Head of nursing				
Inside "look" of facility				
Cleanliness				
Music				
Outings suited for our loved one				
Religious services				
Clothing/possession handling				
Comments in parking lot				
Location of nurse stations				
Resident appearance				
Appearance of rooms				
Smell inside				
Comments of local associations that visit (like Alzheimer's Association)				
Comments of ministers if available				
Nurse focus: residents vs. paper				
"Feel" of residents' "hope"				
Food reports from residents				
Number of visitors allowed				
Proximity, convenience				
Comments of other families				
Feeling of positive attitude				
Variety of fun				
24/7 access				
Your access to staff and other patients				
How medicine is dispensed				
Noise level				
Phone access				
Billing/finance				
Interactions observed				

Evaluate the Facilities

No facility is going to be perfect, but perhaps this checklist will help. Put a + for a positive "feeling" on this item, a − if you had a negative feeling, and a 0 for neutral. Then compare notes with any other siblings who take the time to do the same. If your parents are suddenly in need of a care facility, take your best guess, go for it, and do research for an alternative later. Whatever you do, don't feel you can't make a change.

Facility 1: _____

Facility 2: _____

Facility 3: _____

Facility 4: _____

Item	1	2	3	4
Outside area for walking				
Director of facility				
Head of nursing				
Inside "look" of facility				
Cleanliness				
Music				
Outings suited for our loved one				
Religious services				
Clothing/possession handling				
Comments in parking lot				
Location of nurse stations				
Resident appearance				
Appearance of rooms				
Smell inside				
Comments of local associations that visit (like Alzheimer's Association)				
Comments of ministers if available				
Nurse focus: residents vs. paper				
"Feel" of residents' "hope"				
Food reports from residents				
Number of visitors allowed				
Proximity, convenience				
Comments of other families				
Feeling of positive attitude				
Variety of fun				
24/7 access				
Your access to staff and other patients				
How medicine is dispensed				
Noise level				
Phone access				
Billing/finance				
Interactions observed				

Evaluate the Facilities

No facility is going to be perfect, but perhaps this checklist will help. Put a + for a positive "feeling" on this item, a — if you had a negative feeling, and a 0 for neutral. Then compare notes with any other siblings who take the time to do the same. If your parents are suddenly in need of a care facility, take your best guess, go for it, and do research for an alternative later. Whatever you do, don't feel you can't make a change.

Facility 1: _____

Facility 2: _____

Facility 3: _____

Facility 4: _____

Item	1	2	3	4
Outside area for walking				
Director of facility				
Head of nursing				
Inside "look" of facility				
Cleanliness				
Music				
Outings suited for our loved one				
Religious services				
Clothing/possession handling				
Comments in parking lot				
Location of nurse stations				
Resident appearance				
Appearance of rooms				
Smell inside				
Comments of local associations that visit (like Alzheimer's Association)				
Comments of ministers if available				
Nurse focus: residents vs. paper				
"Feel" of residents' "hope"				
Food reports from residents				
Number of visitors allowed				
Proximity, convenience				
Comments of other families				
Feeling of positive attitude				
Variety of fun				
24/7 access				
Your access to staff and other patients				
How medicine is dispensed				
Noise level				
Phone access				
Billing/finance				
Interactions observed				

Do What You're Good At

(Who is *best* at this in the family? Second best?
Insert initials in those boxes, and then compare notes!)

Name/Initial _____ Name/Initial _____
Name/Initial _____ Name/Initial _____
Name/Initial _____ Name/Initial _____

Skill	Best	Next best	Skill	Best	Next best
Shopping			Trusted by others		
Negotiating			Running errands		
Following up			Creative activities		
Mom's favorite			Has time		
Dad's favorite			Simplifying information		
Documenting records			Teller/reader of family or other stories		
Security/privacy/computers			Noticing problems/details		
Inspiring others			Calling extended family		
Objective view of family			Visiting/chatting		
Completing what's started			Making difficult decisions		
Crafts/clothing care			Event/occasion planning		
Choosing thoughtful gifts			Medical knowledge		
Making phone calls			Financial planning		
Knowledge of family history			Other business and finance matters		
Legal knowledge			Handling emergencies		
Family comic/entertainer			Other		

Date of family meeting _____
Family member filling out form _____
Location _____

Do What You're Good At

(Who is *best* at this in the family? Second best?
Insert initials in those boxes, and then compare notes!)

Name/Initial _____   Name/Initial _____
Name/Initial _____   Name/Initial _____
Name/Initial _____   Name/Initial _____

Skill	Best	Next best	Skill	Best	Next best
Shopping			Trusted by others		
Negotiating			Running errands		
Following up			Creative activities		
Mom's favorite			Has time		
Dad's favorite			Simplifying information		
Documenting records			Teller/reader of family or other stories		
Security/privacy/computers			Noticing problems/details		
Inspiring others			Calling extended family		
Objective view of family			Visiting/chatting		
Completing what's started			Making difficult decisions		
Crafts/clothing care			Event/occasion planning		
Choosing thoughtful gifts			Medical knowledge		
Making phone calls			Financial planning		
Knowledge of family history			Other business and finance matters		
Legal knowledge			Handling emergencies		
Family comic/entertainer			Other		

Date of family meeting _____
Family member filling out form _____
Location _____

Do What You're Good At

(Who is *best* at this in the family? Second best?
Insert initials in those boxes, and then compare notes!)

Name/Initial _____ Name/Initial _____
Name/Initial _____ Name/Initial _____
Name/Initial _____ Name/Initial _____

Skill	Best	Next best	Skill	Best	Next best
Shopping			Trusted by others		
Negotiating			Running errands		
Following up			Creative activities		
Mom's favorite			Has time		
Dad's favorite			Simplifying information		
Documenting records			Teller/reader of family or other stories		
Security/privacy/computers			Noticing problems/details		
Inspiring others			Calling extended family		
Objective view of family			Visiting/chatting		
Completing what's started			Making difficult decisions		
Crafts/clothing care			Event/occasion planning		
Choosing thoughtful gifts			Medical knowledge		
Making phone calls			Financial planning		
Knowledge of family history			Other business and finance matters		
Legal knowledge			Handling emergencies		
Family comic/entertainer			Other		

Date of family meeting _____
Family member filling out form _____
Location _____

Do What You're Good At

(Who is *best* at this in the family? Second best?
Insert initials in those boxes, and then compare notes!)

Name/Initial _____ Name/Initial _____
Name/Initial _____ Name/Initial _____
Name/Initial _____ Name/Initial _____

Skill	Best	Next best	Skill	Best	Next best
Shopping			Trusted by others		
Negotiating			Running errands		
Following up			Creative activities		
Mom's favorite			Has time		
Dad's favorite			Simplifying information		
Documenting records			Teller/reader of family or other stories		
Security/privacy/computers			Noticing problems/details		
Inspiring others			Calling extended family		
Objective view of family			Visiting/chatting		
Completing what's started			Making difficult decisions		
Crafts/clothing care			Event/occasion planning		
Choosing thoughtful gifts			Medical knowledge		
Making phone calls			Financial planning		
Knowledge of family history			Other business and finance matters		
Legal knowledge			Handling emergencies		
Family comic/entertainer			Other		

Date of family meeting _____
Family member filling out form _____
Location _____

Caring for the Caregiver

Year _____   Location _____

Family member filling out form _____

Action Item	Date Done
Called to tell them we appreciate what they are doing	
Called to tell them we appreciate what they are doing	
Called to tell them we appreciate what they are doing	
Called to tell them we appreciate what they are doing	
Called to tell them we appreciate what they are doing	
Called to tell them we appreciate what they are doing	
Called to tell them we appreciate what they are doing	
Called to tell them we appreciate what they are doing	
Called to tell them we appreciate what they are doing	
Called to tell them we appreciate what they are doing	
Called director of facility	
Called director of facility	
Called director of facility	
Sent candy or gifts to staff	
Sent candy or gifts to staff	
Sent candy or gifts to staff	
Came to town and totally "relieved"	
Came to town and totally "relieved"	
Came to town and totally "relieved"	
Called parent and then called caregiver to give them a break from making that call	
Called parent and then called caregiver to give them a break from making that call	
Called parent and then called caregiver to give them a break from making that call	

Caring for the Caregiver

Year _____   Location _____

Family member filling out form _____

Action Item	Date Done
Called to tell them we appreciate what they are doing	
Called to tell them we appreciate what they are doing	
Called to tell them we appreciate what they are doing	
Called to tell them we appreciate what they are doing	
Called to tell them we appreciate what they are doing	
Called to tell them we appreciate what they are doing	
Called to tell them we appreciate what they are doing	
Called to tell them we appreciate what they are doing	
Called to tell them we appreciate what they are doing	
Called to tell them we appreciate what they are doing	
Called director of facility	
Called director of facility	
Called director of facility	
Sent candy or gifts to staff	
Sent candy or gifts to staff	
Sent candy or gifts to staff	
Came to town and totally "relieved"	
Came to town and totally "relieved"	
Came to town and totally "relieved"	
Called parent and then called caregiver to give them a break from making that call	
Called parent and then called caregiver to give them a break from making that call	
Called parent and then called caregiver to give them a break from making that call	

Caring for the Caregiver

Year _____   Location _____

Family member filling out form _____

Action Item	Date Done
Called to tell them we appreciate what they are doing	
Called to tell them we appreciate what they are doing	
Called to tell them we appreciate what they are doing	
Called to tell them we appreciate what they are doing	
Called to tell them we appreciate what they are doing	
Called to tell them we appreciate what they are doing	
Called to tell them we appreciate what they are doing	
Called to tell them we appreciate what they are doing	
Called to tell them we appreciate what they are doing	
Called to tell them we appreciate what they are doing	
Called director of facility	
Called director of facility	
Called director of facility	
Sent candy or gifts to staff	
Sent candy or gifts to staff	
Sent candy or gifts to staff	
Came to town and totally "relieved"	
Came to town and totally "relieved"	
Came to town and totally "relieved"	
Called parent and then called caregiver to give them a break from making that call	
Called parent and then called caregiver to give them a break from making that call	
Called parent and then called caregiver to give them a break from making that call	

Caring for the Caregiver

Year _____   Location _____

Family member filling out form _____

Action Item	Date Done
Called to tell them we appreciate what they are doing	
Called to tell them we appreciate what they are doing	
Called to tell them we appreciate what they are doing	
Called to tell them we appreciate what they are doing	
Called to tell them we appreciate what they are doing	
Called to tell them we appreciate what they are doing	
Called to tell them we appreciate what they are doing	
Called to tell them we appreciate what they are doing	
Called to tell them we appreciate what they are doing	
Called to tell them we appreciate what they are doing	
Called director of facility	
Called director of facility	
Called director of facility	
Sent candy or gifts to staff	
Sent candy or gifts to staff	
Sent candy or gifts to staff	
Came to town and totally "relieved"	
Came to town and totally "relieved"	
Came to town and totally "relieved"	
Called parent and then called caregiver to give them a break from making that call	
Called parent and then called caregiver to give them a break from making that call	
Called parent and then called caregiver to give them a break from making that call	

Caring for the Caregiver

Year _____   Location _____

Family member filling out form _____

Action Item	Date Done
Called to tell them we appreciate what they are doing	
Called to tell them we appreciate what they are doing	
Called to tell them we appreciate what they are doing	
Called to tell them we appreciate what they are doing	
Called to tell them we appreciate what they are doing	
Called to tell them we appreciate what they are doing	
Called to tell them we appreciate what they are doing	
Called to tell them we appreciate what they are doing	
Called to tell them we appreciate what they are doing	
Called to tell them we appreciate what they are doing	
Called director of facility	
Called director of facility	
Called director of facility	
Sent candy or gifts to staff	
Sent candy or gifts to staff	
Sent candy or gifts to staff	
Came to town and totally "relieved"	
Came to town and totally "relieved"	
Came to town and totally "relieved"	
Called parent and then called caregiver to give them a break from making that call	
Called parent and then called caregiver to give them a break from making that call	
Called parent and then called caregiver to give them a break from making that call	